The Ann Person™ Method
Sewing Book #1

Published by Stretch & Sew, Inc., Eugene, Oregon.

Third Edition
First Printing

Contents

About the Author

Although Ann Person's childhood was filled with dreams of success, she never dreamed her success would be measured by a franchise organization that reaches from the Pacific to the Atlantic Oceans.

Born and raised in logging communities near Eugene, Oregon, Ann was reared on the American ethic that prosperity can be achieved through inspiration and hard work. Today, she is the dynamic president of Stretch & Sew, Inc., a multimillion dollar home sewing business.

Ann's journey from logging camp to boardroom included many rough years. She attended the University of Oregon as an art major, but her studies were interrupted during World War II when Ann joined the WACs and taught painting in a convalescent hospital.

After the war Ann returned to the University to continue her studies in Art and Education, which were interrupted when she met Marine Captain Herbert Person. Soon married, they purchased a small resort in an Oregon rural community and became business partners. Within three years they found they had lost $10,000, brought two daughters into the world, and Ann had suffered polio.

Herb began to search for a way to keep the family together and to save the property they owned. With the purchase of a horse and a hand-falling saw, Herb started a company that became a very successful logging operation. Ann devoted her time to raising their daughters Claudia and Kris, and a third daughter Mindy was born.

In 1956, Herb was injured in a logging accident. Following a year of convalescence in Arizona, he moved the family back to Oregon to find that the partners in the logging operation had lost all of the business that he had built up. The Persons were going to have to start over again.

The first attempt at recovery was a vitamin sales organization, requiring both Herb and Ann to sell vitamins door to door. After this failed, a Cessna Aviation business was started, again unsuccessful. Herb soon found himself working as a salesman for a company that he had previously sold an airplane to. Ann found work as a saleslady for the Singer Sewing Machine Company, but that was brought to an abrupt halt when she suffered an automobile accident that incapacitated her for two years. After recovering from the accident, Ann returned to Singer, teaching sewing classes including a series of teen classes.

Not yet busy enough, Ann branched out from Singer to travel around Oregon, giving antiquing demonstrations in hardware stores. She started a painting class at a parks and recreation center, taught resin casting classes for a paint store, and made picture frames for students (as well as for her own paintings which she regularly sold).

One day a neighbor asked Ann to give a teen sewing class at the parks and recreation center where she taught painting. Ann agreed on the condition that she could teach the teens a new method of sewing she had developed by trial and error. The new method involved using knit fabrics and new techniques rather than the old-fashioned ways she had taught at Singer. The mothers readily agreed since they were more interested in keeping their girls busy rather than in what sewing method would be taught.

The classes were a smash from the beginning. The girls learned, just as Ann had thought they would, because sewing with knit fabrics was exceptionally easy. Ann had the ability to teach her method in such a way that the girls suddenly discovered a whole new world of sewing. They were creating their own T-shirts as well as sewing for their families.

The mothers were delighted, to say the least, and they soon asked Ann to share her secrets with them. Ann made arrangements with a local fabric shop, started her famous lessons, and gave them the name of *Stretch & Sew*®. By the fall of 1966, Ann found herself traveling through the states of Oregon, Washington and California, teaching seemingly unending groups of women her wonderful method.

From the first, Ann was frustrated because the major pattern companies had not yet realized that special patterns were necessary to sew efficiently with knit fabrics. So to solve her problem, Ann started cutting her own patterns from butcher paper and selling them to her students. In February of 1967, Ann had her first patterns printed.

By August, Ann had opened a little knit fabric shop in Eugene, Oregon, and trained teachers to teach her method. It had become quite apparent that she could not personally teach every one who wanted to learn about this wonderful new method of sewing.

In September of that same year, Ann wrote a book on sewing with knits. She wrote in longhand and drew illustrations as a friend typed and edited. Ann worried about whether or not it would sell. To her surprise and delight, it was a best seller and became one of the most important parts of her marketing plan. Today her book has sold over 1,000,000 copies.

In June of 1968, Herb decided that the business had grown beyond Ann's ability to manage alone. He left his position as Vice President of Operations for Willamette Valley Company and joined Ann to develop a franchising company that was to grow beyond either of their wildest dreams.

Ann didn't just have a desire to share her knowledge of sewing with her students. She realized that to create all of the wonderful looks that are found in ready-to-wear,

it would be necessary to carry many of the trims that are used in manufacturing. Soon she had trims dyed to coordinate with her fabrics.

For the first time, a marketing system was developed that offers the home sewer a totally coordinated collection of fabrics, trims, and patterns. Today each fabric for sale in a *Stretch & Sew Fabrics*® center has been carefully selected to be sure that the weight, stretch and color are perfect for the garment it is designed to create. Patterns are tested on fabrics and often designed with special fabrics in mind. Never in the history of sewing has so much painstaking work gone into establishing a total sewing center.

New techniques are continually being developed to add to the first sewing tips Ann developed. She is still delighted when she discovers another new technique to help cut sewing time to half that of ordinary sewing. The *Ann Person*™ Method of sewing still delights everyone who learns its secrets.

Ann feels that much of her success in this wonderful business is due to the fact that she is really one of her own best customers. She finds that she can relate to her customers very easily and understand their needs. You see, Ann is still a home seamstress. With all of her success in the business world, sewing is still her first and best love.

Her greatest thrill today is to see women like herself realizing their own potential. These are women who never dreamed that they could own and operate their own business. Through their love of sewing and their excitement in sharing her method with others, they have opened their own franchised stores to become successful in their own right.

Introduction to the Third Edition

This book and your *Stretch & Sew*® sewing classes are my ways of sharing with you my *Ann Person*™ Method of sewing. I've been teaching my method for years now, and I find that Stretch & Sew customers are continually delighted to learn such simple ways to sew such professional-looking garments. But my techniques are not static. Over the years, they've been refined, and I'm always thrilled when I discover yet another way to cut down the time of sewing.

One of the things that inspired me to start developing my *Ann Person*™ Method of sewing was that I had three teenage daughters and I wanted them to love sewing as much as I do. I realized that if I could teach my daughters how to sew with knits, I could get them really thrilled about sewing because the techniques I had developed for knits over the years were so fast and simple. I knew that if you give someone a project that can be accomplished quickly and easily, you create in that person a desire to learn more.

And so that is how it occurred to me to teach the very first class I ever taught on sewing with knits. My daughter Kris helped me with the class which was held at a parks and recreation center. I borrowed sewing machines to teach a group of about ten young teenagers how to make a knit top. They loved the miracle of using ribbing to sew neckbands on their tops.

That first class was certainly rough in its methodology. I recall sewing the crew neckband to a knit top and not being able to get the top over a girl's head. Then I realized that all I had to do was cut the neck opening larger and sew the neckband back on to make it the right size. But I was a long way from having the sophisticated techniques I developed later for measuring neck openings and determining the correct length of ribbing for neckbands. Now it's possible to get it right on the first try.

The other part of this class that was exciting to the girls was learning how to stretch a sleeve into a knit top. Over the years this has continued to be one of the most popular of my techniques. Everyone always loves how pretty a stretched-in sleeve looks when it's finished. One of the really important things to me in working out my techniques is that the garment must *really* look professionally done when it's completed. I've always disliked garments that appear home-sewn — that have the look of "tender, loving hands at home."

When I was a young girl, my mother sewed most of my clothes for me because we were very poor and, of necessity, they were usually made from old things of hers which she had taken apart. I can remember one of my great wishes was to be able to buy a ready-made coat. I became determined that if I were going to sew, I would find ways to sew so the clothing I made would be clothing I would be really proud to wear.

I began working out my techniques as I sewed for my daughters. I can remember that when the girls bought a garment they would want to cut the label out so that no one would know it was ready-made. To them it was very much of a status symbol to be able to say that their mother made the lovely outfits they wore.

So I achieved both goals that I had hoped to achieve. First I developed a method of sewing that's easy and fast. In fact, I feel the techniques I teach will cut the time of ordinary sewing in half. But, also, my method makes it possible for you to create really lovely-looking garments. Now your friends won't say, "Oh, my dear, did you make your dress?" Instead they will say, "You didn't make that?"

vi

Basic Principles

Introduction

When I developed the sewing techniques you will learn in your classes, I never imagined they would become the foundation of a large and successful company, Stretch & Sew. It just happened that as I worked out methods for sewing with knits, I was discovering a way to increase the satisfaction of sewing for everyone. I wasn't alone in wanting to complete a garment in half the time of ordinary sewing. Or in wanting my clothing to look as fashionable as the finest couture designers'.

These classes and this sewing book are my ways of sharing with you what I've discovered. You will learn my *Ann Person*™ sewing techniques step by step as you sew the garments for your classes. Let me stress here the importance of actually sewing each garment as you are introduced to it. To learn new techniques, you must do them — and it is far easier while the information is fresh in your mind. Meanwhile, this chapter will provide a background before you begin sewing with knits.

Basic Principles

Patterns

Fashion Patterns

Let me introduce you to *Stretch & Sew®* patterns, which I design exclusively for knit fabrics. In your classes you will be working with basic patterns for classic garments. You will learn the fundamentals in pattern adjustments and sewing techniques which apply to all *Stretch & Sew* patterns.

At your *Stretch & Sew Fabrics®* center, there will always be new patterns reflecting the very latest in design. Many of these fashion patterns are MAKE-IT-IN-MINUTES™ patterns like the ones you'll work with during your classes.

Master Pattern Concept

Stretch & Sew patterns combine the best elements of pattern-making with a unique feature. You see, every *Stretch & Sew* pattern is a master pattern which means that a range of sizes has been printed on each pattern.

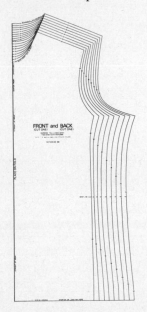

FRONT and BACK
(CUT ONE) (CUT ONE)

This gives you the advantage of being able to use the same master pattern for several people. An even greater advantage is that you are able to achieve a custom fit by using a combination of pattern sizes. It still excites me to think of how helpful *Stretch & Sew* patterns have been to the home sewer for this reason. If one of the motivations for sewing is to escape the standard sizing of the ready-to-wear industry, how can sewing be any better unless the pattern makes it possible to avoid the same standard sizing?

Stretch & Sew patterns are sized according to body measurements. Tops, dresses, and shirts are sized by bust or chest measurement, and skirts and pants are sized by hip measurement.

The size range for each pattern is indicated on the front of the envelope along with "views" of the garments featured in the pattern. On the back of the envelope is a yardage chart, a listing of notions required, and the recommended fabrics for the pattern — all the information you need to leave your *Stretch & Sew Fabrics* center prepared to sew.

On the back of the envelope you will also find the Standard Body Measurements Chart and the Finished Garment Measurements Chart. In your classes you will learn how to use these charts to get a good fit. May I stress here the importance of taking accurate body measurements — when you select a size, be sure you have chosen the size you are today and not the size you once were or hope to be in the future.

Tracing Your Pattern

Each *Stretch & Sew* pattern is printed on a permanent sheet to create a master pattern. Keep the master pattern intact. Instead of cutting it, you will trace a personal pattern, using *Perky®* pattern paper or *Do-Sew®* tracing material. You will be introduced to these two Stretch & Sew products in Class 1 as you learn the most efficient way to go about preparing your personal pattern.

Pattern Adjustments

In your classes you will also learn basic pattern adjustments to make your personal pattern fit your figure. If you're like me, you can literally spend days shopping for pants that fit comfortably and you end up settling for a pair that almost fit but aren't the right color or the right fabric. Class 2 will be your greatest reward. You'll learn how to adjust and fit a pair of pants that will take you one-half hour to sew. The same goes in Class 4 for those of you who have never had a bustline dart fall in the right place for your figure.

Designer Techniques

Equally exciting are the designer techniques you will learn in your classes. For instance, in Class 4 you will not only learn how to apply Chanel trim, but you will also learn the principles for adapting this finish to any pattern you choose. Your satisfaction in sewing will double when you learn the simple tricks necessary to be your own fashion designer.

Fabric

Now, as a confirmed fabriholic, it's my pleasure to introduce you to *Stretch & Sew*® knit fabrics. As I mentioned before, your classes will teach you sewing techniques which will give your clothing a lovely professional appearance. But sewing techniques alone will not do the job. It's also necessary to work with fabrics of the highest quality that are appropriate for the pattern you have selected. And I consider it my business to make such fabrics available to you. In fact, as a home seamstress myself, a woman who has loved to sew all of her life, I feel we have created a fantasy store — a store that fills all of your sewing needs.

In your *Stretch & Sew Fabrics* center, you will find an ever-changing selection of prints, stripes, plaids, and solids which reflect the most current fashions in fabric. These are the fabrics which are seen in fine ready-to-wear for that season. I enjoy a good chuckle whenever I see a lovely dress in one of the world's leading department stores and I realize that the same fabric is available in our *Stretch & Sew*® stores at the same time.

Something else you will appreciate in our fabrics is that they are color-coordinated. Planning a spring/summer or fall/winter wardrobe is easy to do and it's exciting because of the mix and match possibilities.

Fabric Selection

Your choice of fabrics for your sewing is as varied as knits themselves. During your classes, you will learn the fundamental properties of knit fabrics to help you achieve the results you want in your finished garment. There are several basic things you will want to consider.

Important to the finished appearance of your garment are the weight and "hand" of the fabric. How does it feel when you hold it? Firm? Soft? Light? Textured? Smooth? Select a fabric that will lend itself to the desired look you wish to achieve in your finished garment.

The fit of a garment is affected by the stretch of the fabric. Most *Stretch & Sew* patterns are designed for fabric that has 25 percent stretch, but some fabrics have more or less stretch. In Chapter Two you will learn a simple technique for determining percent of stretch, and in Chapter Three you will learn how to adjust your pattern to accommodate varying degrees of stretch.

Wearing and care characteristics of a fabric are dependent on the fiber content as well as on the knit stitch the fabric is constructed in. At your *Stretch & Sew Fabrics* center, you will find a Care Instruction number on each bolt end designated by our Quality Control Department. This number is your key to specific instructions on caring for the fabric.

Pretreating Fabric

Probably one of the most exciting features of sewing your own knit top is the fact that you will wash the fabric before you cut and sew it. I'm sure you have all at one time or another splurged on a pretty cotton knit top only to have it shrink in the dryer — and it shrank in a most peculiar way so you ended up with a short, fat little top. The opposite frustration is spending time to line-dry even your everyday sportswear.

For consistently good results, you should pretreat all your fabric. The rule is: *Treat your fabric before it is cut as you will treat the finished garment*

If you plan to wash your garment in hot water and dry it on a hot setting in your dryer, you must wash the fabric in hot water and dry it on the hot setting in your dryer. Remember to use soap or detergent in this first washing to remove any excess dye that could be on the fabric. Do not mix light-colored fabrics with dark-colored fabrics because they might pick up color.

One *exception* to the rule on pretreating is ribbing which is the trim you will use on your T-shirts for Class 1. You should *not* pretreat ribbing unless you have selected a darker color such as red or navy for trim to be used with a light-colored fabric. In this case, you would pretreat in order to remove any residual dye on the ribbing — but do it *after* cutting the trim to the correct length.

Cutting Techniques

Will It Run?

To the most frequently asked question, "But, if I cut it, won't it run?", my answer is no. Double knits do not run, and most other knits have been processed to prevent running. In addition to this, many of the synthetic yarns are texturized which causes a meshing of the stitches to discourage running.

Occasionally, a nylon or polyester yarn that has been designed to have a very silky appearance will have a tendency to run when stress is applied to the cut edge. However, if the fabric is handled with care, running will not occur. Generally, these knits will only run in one direction. Check the fabric you are going to be working with. If it has a tendency to run, place all the pattern pieces in the same direction so that the "running edge" will be at the bottom edge of the garment where there's less stress and where the hem will seal the yarns.

Permanent Crease

Check the crease in the fabric. Sometimes this crease is pressed in during the manufacturing process and becomes permanent. Whenever a fabric has been finished in a tube, the crease will be permanent. Even a cotton stripe that comes in a tube stitched along one side will have a fold that cannot be removed. To avoid a permanent crease, simply refold the fabric so the crease falls at the edge of the garment pieces rather than through the center. The permanent crease can be used down the center of a sleeve.

Pattern Layout

Some fabrics have a raised surface which is brushed in one direction, creating a nap. When you are cutting napped fabrics, the pattern pieces must be laid so the nap runs the same way — either up or down — in all parts of the finished garment. Otherwise, the shading in the fabric will not be the same throughout the garment. I always cut velour and corduroy with the nap running up to create a rich depth to the color of the fabric. The choice is yours — just be sure you are consistent as colors can change greatly when a nap is involved.

A simple test for nap is to machine-baste two swatches of the fabric together in opposite directions. Press the seam and hold the swatches up to the light for a close inspection. If no difference in shading appears, you may cut the fabric either way. Many prints have a one-way design which must be treated in the same way as a napped fabric. In fact, I recommend you make a habit of laying your pattern pieces in the same direction unless you have made a test seam.

When you sew with knits, the pattern pieces should be placed on the fabric so that the greater amount of stretch goes across the pattern. This means that the greater amount of stretch will go around the body in the finished garment. Check the stretch in your fabric and place the pattern pieces according to this rule.

Of course, there are exceptions to every rule. When you are working with a border design, for instance, it will often be necessary to ignore the stretch rule to create a special effect. The advantage here is that this styling is usually seen on a fuller skirt and the stretch will not affect the fit.

Your Sewing Machine

What Kind of Machine?

Nearly all of my sewing techniques can be readily and properly accomplished on any sewing machine, including the reliable old treadle machine rarely found in homes today. Sewing with knit fabrics wouldn't be so popular if this were not true. For some garments, a zigzag stitch on your machine makes sewing easier and adds stretchability when you apply elastic.

Your sewing machine should be kept in absolutely tip-top condition. Oil your machine regularly and remove dust and lint to keep the parts moving freely. Consult your sewing machine manual for specific care instructions and, also, to learn how to take full advantage of the features of your sewing machine. If it is not stitching evenly, have your dealer balance the tension.

Sewing Machine Needles

Most sewing machines manufactured in the past twenty-five years have been designed to take standard-sized needles. Needle sizes that we use in our knit sewing are 9, 11, and 14. Size 9 is the smallest while size 14 is the largest. Size 11 is the size used for most of our sewing.

To compare domestic and European needle sizes, refer to the following chart:

American Size	European Size
9	65
11	75
14	90

We recommend sewing knits with a ball point needle. A ball point needle has a straighter shank and a slightly rounded end, enabling it to enter the fabric without breaking the fibers. Ball point needles have the additional advantage of discouraging skipped stitches.

Changing the needle often is an essential part of sewing satisfactorily on knits. The rounded end of the needle is gradually dulled while you sew, losing its effectiveness in protecting the fabric.

A needle with a slight burr on the end will cause little holes to appear along the seamline. The most common cause of a burr on the end of a needle is hitting a pin while you sew. I suggest you check for these rough edges by drawing the needle — even a new needle — through your thumb and forefinger. Also, check the end of the needle to make sure the point is intact.

Stitch Length

Knit sewing requires a wide range of stitch lengths from the long, machine-basting stitch to the small stitches used for sewing stays in place. Domestic sewing machines usually have a stitch length regulator which indicates stitches per inch. However, the stitch length regulators on many European brand sewing machines are labelled with the numbers 0, 1, 2, 3, 4. These numbers are based on metric measurements. A setting of 1, for example, indicates that the stitch is one millimeter long. A setting of 4 indicates that the stitch is 4 millimeters long.

The following chart indicates the satisfactory stitch length for most purposes in our sewing. To avoid confusion, you may wish to copy the chart and keep it handy for reference as you sew.

Stitches per Inch	Millimeter Stitch Length	Uses
6	4	Decorative topstitching, basting, and gathering
9	3	The normal stitch for knits
12	2.5	For stays and reinforcement stitching

Sewing Seams

Seam Allowances

The seam allowances on *Stretch & Sew* patterns are usually ⅝ inch (1.6 cm) or ¼ inch (0.6 cm) wide. The appropriate seam allowance for a pattern is determined partly by the design of the garment. Also, a pattern may be intended for a particular category of fabrics which sews up more easily with the narrower or the wider seam allowance. In any case, make a habit of checking the seam allowance given on a pattern each time you begin to sew.

Beginning Your Seam

Nothing is more frustrating than having your sewing machine jam as you start a seam. Jamming is caused when the upper and lower threads have been carried down into the hole in the throat plate. Soft knits also have a tendency to be drawn into the needle hole. Both instances can be avoided by holding the upper and lower threads with your left hand for the first few stitches, keeping a slight amount of pull on the threads. This will ensure that the fabric will feed through the machine evenly from the start.

One of my most terrifying moments was a live television show I did in Boston, Massachusetts, a few years ago. The studio was in an uproar before we went on the air and I felt thoroughly confused. I was sewing a sweater on the program and, sure enough, I did just what I told you not to do — I forgot to hold on to the threads. After a few stitches, I knew I was in trouble. So I decided that since it was a live show, my only hope was to pull the fabric free. It was my lucky day — it came out and I smiled at my audience and said, "I have just done what you should not do." Then I proceeded to sew the seam properly. But I will never forget the fantasies I had of spending seven minutes on live television with a jammed sewing machine.

So, if the machine is not feeding the fabric ahead, stop quickly. The more stitches you pound into that hole, the harder it is going to be to get your fabric free.

Also, when you sew, make it a practice to backstitch at the beginning and end of each seam. To backstitch, insert the needle into the fabric ½ inch (1.3 cm) from the beginning of the seam. Reverse-stitch to the beginning point, and then stitch forward exactly over the reverse-stitching. This will secure the threads and prevent the seam from coming out.

Stretching As You Sew

For most of our sewing, we use a straight stitch. This stitch has many advantages, but unlike a zigzag stitch, it does not build stretch into a seam. Therefore, one of our most important techniques and one which you will not find in any other type of sewing is the principle of *stretching* the fabric as you sew with a straight stitch. This will give the seam the same elasticity that the knit fabric itself has.

Preventing Skipped Stitches

If your sewing machine is skipping stitches, hold the fabric taut to prevent it from clinging to the needle. When the fabric clings to the needle, it holds the thread up so that it isn't picked up by the hook on the bobbin assembly and this causes a skipped stitch.

A residue may build up on the needle when you've been sewing with synthetic fabrics, causing the fabric to cling to the needle. Simply remove the residue by cleaning the needle with rubbing alcohol.

Sometimes, when you are working with very closely knit fabric, your machine may persist in skipping stitches. In this case, I recommend that you switch to a smaller size needle. A finer needle will be able to penetrate the fabric more easily without clinging, eliminating the cause of the skipped stitches.

You may find that your machine regularly skips stitches, even on normal double knits. This is an indication that the timing is off, and you should take the machine to your dealer for repair.

Pressing Techniques

The Importance of Pressing

Pressing is a must for a beautifully finished garment. Any knit except sweater fabric benefits from pressing, and this pressing must be a part of construction — not a last minute thought after you complete the garment. Every seam should be pressed right after you sew it.

Using a Press Cloth

The secret to pressing wool and synthetics effectively without damaging the fabric is to use a damp press cloth which protects the fibers and provides steam to achieve the necessary temperature. The type of press cloth you use is a matter of personal preference as long as you use one which is absorbent. The moisture is necessary to provide adequate steam for pressing knits. I prefer a square of white cotton interlock. For more convenience in pressing, I keep a bowl of water at my ironing board to use when the cloth needs additional dampening.

A cotton ironing board cover also helps to protect fabric. The cotton absorbs the heat instead of reflecting it back. If the heat is reflected back, the temperature may build until it is too hot for your fabric.

Pressing Acrylics

Care must be taken when pressing acrylics. The moment steam hits acrylic fibers, they relax and easily stretch out of shape. So, keep the garment from hanging over the side of the ironing board or the steamed area will stretch. You should also allow the garment to cool before you move it from the ironing board. Incidentally, new body will be given to acrylic by pressing with a damp cloth until the cloth is dry.

Creasing and Shaping Your Fabric

Women are amazed when I tell them that it is possible to permanently press the crease in a pair of pants when they are made of a polyester or wool double knit. These fabrics also press well enough to use with a pattern that requires a sharply pressed pleat. The steam from a damp cloth and a warm iron (wool setting) is all that is necessary.

When you are working with polyester or wool knit fabrics, you can use a steam iron and damp cloth to shape collars, lapels and hems. For example, a hem with a good amount of flare can be eased with a damp cloth and a fairly warm iron. The fullness will ease into itself, giving a beautiful flat surface for hemming.

Sewing Aids

The Importance of Sewing Aids

With the growth of Stretch & Sew, I have realized a dream of providing a total sewing center. The quality, color-coordinated fabrics, the master patterns, and the sewing classes are part of that picture. The sewing notions and tools we carry are also important. They are designed to save you time and to help you achieve a professional finish in your garments. Study the notion racks to discover the new ideas continually available. Put them to work for you.

Now, let me introduce you to some of the products you'll be using in your classes.

Tape Measure

A tape measure is a necessity for sewing and the *Stretch & Sew*™ tape measure is as durable and reliable as they come. It is made of fiber glass so it won't stretch, and it may be washed without shrinking. Dimensions in inches are printed on both sides, beginning at opposite ends of the tape measure. So, you can start measuring with whichever end you happen to pick up. Metric dimensions are also provided.

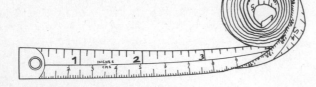

Perky Pattern Paper

As I mentioned before, you will learn to trace a personal pattern from *Stretch & Sew* master patterns. *Perky* pattern paper is my favorite tracing material. We had it the first year of Stretch & Sew and we've used it ever since.

Perky pattern paper is easy to mark on, especially with a felt tip pen. It has dots approximately 1 inch (2.5 cm) apart which are helpful in making pattern adjustments — although I recommend a ruler for precise measuring.

If I am doing any creating at all, I always make my first pattern on the dotted paper. Once I have a final pattern, I transfer it to *Do-Sew*.

Do-Sew

Do-Sew is a synthetic tracing material which folds compactly and presses easily. Because it's so durable and long-lasting, as well as easy to store, it's handy for favorite patterns which you plan to use again and again. *Do-Sew* is also used as a stay fabric.

Pattern Weights

Stretch & Sew™ pattern weights hold your tracing material in place as you trace your pattern and cut your fabric. They're quicker than pins and more convenient than the salt and pepper shakers I used years ago.

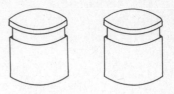

Clear Plastic Rulers

Clear plastic rulers are indispensable for making pattern adjustments. Also, you can trace your patterns much more quickly and accurately if you use the edge of a ruler as a guide. For your sewing, I recommend both a straightedge ruler and a curved fashion ruler.

Cutting Boards

A cutting board will provide a large flat surface to make it easier for you to trace your patterns and cut your fabric. A cutting board is easy to pin to and it's marked for accurate measuring. It will protect your table tops and floors from the nicks of scissors or pins. And, it folds up for easy storage.

Fabric Marker

A *Stretch & Sew*™ fabric marker provides the easiest and safest way to transfer construction marks to your fabric. You no longer have to worry about poking holes in your fabric with a tracing wheel or leaving permanent marks from other marking tools. You simply wipe away the ink from the *Stretch & Sew* fabric marker, using a cloth thoroughly moistened with plain water. It's important, however, that you wipe away the ink with water *before* you launder the garment.

Shears

It would be impossible for me to stress enough the importance of having sharp shears with a good point. They are a must if you're going to cut your fabric easily and accurately. When you are buying new shears, test several pairs to find the size that's comfortable for you.

Incidentally, the distinction between shears and scissors has to do with the position of the handle in relation to the blades. When you're cutting with shears, it's easier to hold the blades level with your cutting surface.

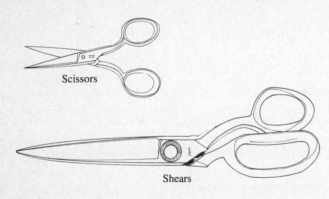

Scissors

Shears

One important tip on cutting is: always look where you are going to cut — out ahead and not at the shears. This will keep you on target. I think of cutting and sewing like driving a car — look where you are going, not where you have been.

Glasshead Pins

Another must for your sewing is *Stretch & Sew*™ glasshead pins. The large heads on these pins increase their visibility and keep them from slipping through the yarns of soft knit fabrics. You will notice that these pins have an extra long shaft which also helps to keep them in place.

Let me emphasize now the importance of removing pins as you sew to prevent damage to your sewing

machine needle. Even if you manage to avoid breaking your needle, sewing over pins will blunt a ball point needle so it will damage your fabric.

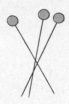

Wrist Pin Cushion

The *Stretch & Sew*™ wrist pin cushion is so much a part of my anatomy that after I have been sewing, I have accidentally worn it out to dinner or to bed! This wrist pin cushion will save you time and frustration as you sew because the pins will always be at hand when you need them. And, the solid back of the cushion will protect your wrist from an accidental jab. WARNING: If you become addicted to a wrist pin cushion, I won't be responsible if you forget to put it on and stick your wrist with a pin!

Ball Point Sewing Machine Needles

Stretch & Sew™ ball point needles are of the finest quality available. As I mentioned before, these needles will separate the yarns, preventing the fibers from being damaged to create holes in your more delicate fabrics. It's important that you change the needle frequently to protect knits.

Thread

There are many fine threads available for your sewing. For sewing on knit fabrics, I recommend threads made either of polyester or of a polyester core with cotton wrapping. The polyester adds strength to the thread which in turn adds strength to your seams. Select a thread in a shade slightly darker than your fabric because, when sewn into a fabric, thread appears lighter than it does on the spool.

Thread Nippers

Stretch & Sew™ thread nippers are a real delight for cutting threads as you sew. Shears, which are designed for cutting fabric, are simply not as convenient to handle while you're sewing. You will find that using thread nippers will speed up your garment construction — you can hold them in one hand to cut the threads quickly. And a built-in spring opens the blades for the next snip.

Sewing Gauge

The *Stretch & Sew*™ sewing gauge is a short ruler with a sliding indicator. You'll find it invaluable for measuring when you press in hems.

Seam Ripper

There isn't a seamstress alive who hasn't had to open a seam for one reason or another, and since this situation is inevitable from time to time, it's vital that you have a very sharp seam ripper. If the seam ripper has become dull, you should purchase a new one. You have to use so much pressure to cut threads with a dull seam ripper that you may damage your fabric unintentionally.

I hope you won't be ripping out too many seams. But when you need to, the *Stretch & Sew*™ seam ripper makes it possible to remove stitches easily. This handy tool also serves as a buttonhole cutter.

Perky Bond® Fusible Web

Perky Bond is an iron-on hemming tape which will save you hours of time and give you a beautiful hem. In Class 2, you will learn the most effective way of applying *Perky Bond* for a hem that will last the lifetime of your garment.

Perky Bond Plus® Fusible Interfacing

Perky Bond Plus is an iron-on interfacing which comes in woven and nonwoven forms to provide the perfect weight interfacing for your garment. This product is so easy to use that you can sew tailored garments with no extra trouble. You will never need to stitch interfacing to the garment pieces again. And you'll never get a homemade look that comes from using an inferior product. You'll learn all you need to know about *Perky Bond Plus* when you sew your tab front shirt in Class 6.

Point Turner

Perfect for turning out corners, especially on collars, the *Stretch & Sew*™ point turner ensures a professional finish to your garment.

Elastic

Stretch & Sew™ elastic comes in two basic forms. There's the braided elastic which we use in a "turned-down" elastic finish for pull-on pants and skirts, swimsuits, and body suits. This elastic has a high degree of stretch. We also have a firmer woven elastic we use for waistbands. Both types of elastic are manufactured to meet Stretch & Sew's quality specifications in order to maintain their stretch through the lifetime of your garment. You'll learn the turned-down elastic finish in Class 2, and you'll learn how to use the woven elastic in Class 7.

It is always the best buy on elastic to purchase from five to ten yards at a time. Then you can cut whatever length you need. Because both elastics are cotton, they will shrink. It is interesting that when the elastic is sewn to an edge and zigzagged, the shrinking does not cause a problem. But if it is going to be loose in a casing, it is imperative that you preshrink the elastic by soaking it in hot water and drying it in the dryer.

I have called this chapter Basic Principles, but you have seen that much of it is really time-saving methods and devices. I am very concerned about the use of my time, and I believe you are too!

Chapter 1
The T-Shirt

Introduction

This knit top is one of the most satisfactory garments you will ever sew. Applying the ribbing to the neck edge is a thrill for a beginning sewer as much as for an expert. There is probably no other sewing experience that will give you as much pleasure as sewing around the circle of the neck opening, stretching the ribbing between the pins as you go, and then removing it from the sewing machine to discover the lovely, soft curve that you've created in the crew neckband of the knit top.

Stretching in a sleeve is another exciting part of sewing this garment. As I think back to my early years of teaching, I remember a Home Economics teacher saying to me, ''Ann, we'll let you come to school and teach a class to the students after we've taught them all the important things that they need to know about sewing.'' This included setting a sleeve in a woven blouse which was difficult for them to do without getting puckers. One of the greatest satisfactions I ever received was showing these students how simple it was to stretch a sleeve into a knit top by simply dividing the sleeve in half, pinning it at the shoulder seam and stretching the garment armhole to fit the sleeve.

In addition to the construction techniques for a knit top, you will learn how to prepare a pattern to fit your figure, and you will learn to cut striped fabric for perfectly matched stripes at all the seams. This is an exciting class which builds the foundation for everything you will be discovering in the classes to come.

The T-Shirt

Pattern Selection

Stretch & Sew® Pattern No. 310

The T-shirt you will be making in Class 1 is from *Stretch & Sew* Pattern No. 310. This pattern features a T-shirt with a crew neckband and a T-shirt with a turtleneck finish. Both may be sewn with short or long sleeves. For your class you will be sewing a crew neck T-shirt, but complete instructions for sewing the turtleneck are included under "Special Information" at the end of this chapter.

Fabric Selection

Stretch & Sew Pattern No. 310 is actually two patterns —one for fabric with 25 percent stretch and one for fabric with 50 percent stretch. This is because the fit of a garment is affected by the amount of stretch in the fabric. In Class 2 you will learn how to test fabric for percent of stretch. For Class 1, all you need to know is that cotton single knit nearly always has 25 percent stretch. Your teacher will help you select a fabric that will work perfectly for your T-shirt.

Stretch & Sew cotton single knits are color-coordinated with the other *Stretch & Sew*® fabrics. As you select your T-shirt fabric, keep in mind the wardrobe you will build as you sew the garments for your classes. I recommend that you choose a striped fabric so that you can practice matching stripes.

Fabric made from cotton is ideal for your T-shirt. It's absorbent and it's soft to the touch, adding greater comfort to an already comfortable garment. You will find that most cotton single knits are blended with polyester. Polyester adds durability and shape-retention to the fabric to keep your T-shirt new-looking through many, many washings. Polyester also resists wrinkles so your T-shirt will stay fresh through the day.

Single knit creates a lightweight fabric which is perfect for the T-shirt. You can recognize a single knit fabric because the knit stitches on the wrong side appear different than they do on the right side. Also, the cut edges of a single knit tend to curl slightly to the right side.

A single knit is knit on a circular machine into a tube. With striped fabric, the tube must be cut open before the garment pieces are cut to make matching possible. In striped fabrics, the tube is cut along one side and re-stitched by the manufacturer to align the stripes which the circular machine knits into a barberpole pattern. In single knits, the folded edges of the tube are permanent creases. When you cut your T-shirt pieces, you will learn how to use these creases.

The crew neckband and the turtleneck for your T-shirts are sewn from what we call "ribbing." This is a very stretchy fabric knit in a rib stitch which creates the same appearance on both sides of the fabric. Ribbing is also knit in a tube which must be opened before you cut your neckline trim. At your *Stretch & Sew Fabrics*® center, you will find ribbing in a rainbow of colors coordinated with all the other fabrics.

Yardage and Notions

After you have selected your fabric, refer to the back of the Pattern No. 310 envelope for yardage and notions. You will notice that 2½ inches (6.4 cm) of ribbing is required for View A, the T-shirt with the crew neckband. When ribbing is sold for neckline trim, it is sold by inches (cm) rather than yards (m) because small quantities are required.

The T-Shirt

Preparing Your Pattern

Determining Your Pattern Size

The first step in preparing your T-shirt pattern is to take the necessary body measurements. Then you will be able to determine your pattern size and to find out whether or not you must make any pattern adjustments to ensure a good fit.

As you take your measurements, hold the tape so it's snug but not tight. You should be able to feel the tape against your body, yet it should be loose enough to slide back and forth. For accurate measurements, I suggest you enlist the help of a friend. And, remember to be honest with yourself when you read the tape. It will pay off in the long run because there's nothing more slimming than a good fit.

Jot down the measurements as you take them. In fact, you may wish to save the list so you won't have to take every measurement each time you sew. But, if you even suspect that you've gained or lost weight or that your measurements have changed, you should measure again before sewing a new garment.

Now refer to the back of the Pattern No. 310 envelope and you will find a Standard Body Measurements Chart. This chart indicates which measurements you should take.

The first measurement on the Standard Body Measurements Chart is for your *bust*. Take this measurement at the fullest part of your bustline.

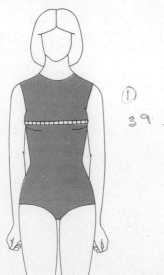

Choose the pattern size that corresponds to your bust measurement. If, for example, your bust measurement is 34 inches (87.0 cm), select size 34 for your T-shirt. If your bust measurement is 38 inches (97.0 cm), select size 38. If the measurement is between sizes, don't worry — I will teach you how to handle this when you trace your pattern pieces.

As you take the following measurements indicated on the Standard Body Measurements Chart, you may find that they do not correspond to the measurements indicated for your size. Again, don't worry. As you do your tracing, you will learn to make simple adjustments to create a pattern to fit your figure. Now take your *waist* measurement.

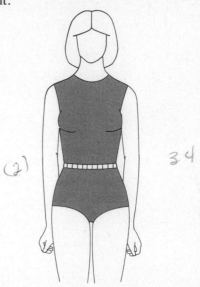

Next measure 9 inches (22.9 cm) below your waistline and take your *hip* measurement.

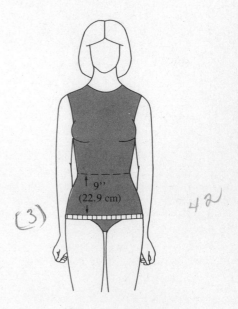

14

Take a *center back waist length* measurement, starting at the cervical bone at the base of your neck and measuring to your waistline as illustrated.

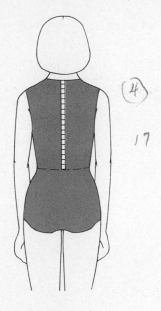

With a slight bend in your elbow, take an *arm length* measurement, starting at your shoulder bone and measuring to your wrist bone.

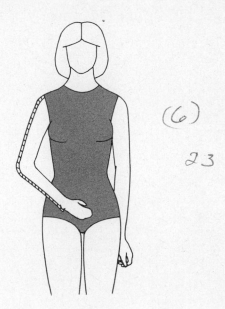

Measure the distance across your back from shoulder bone to shoulder bone. This is called your *"back shoulder width."*

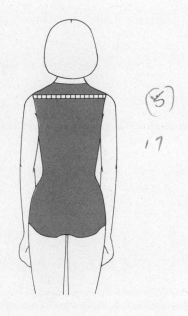

You will notice that there is also a Finished Garment Measurements Chart on the back of the pattern envelope. This chart tells you how long the finished T-shirt will be. For most everyone, the T-shirt will finish at an attractive length as it is designed. Any subtraction or addition in length that may be necessary will be achieved by a center back waist length adjustment to raise or lower the waistline.

Whenever you are sewing pants, skirts, or dresses, however, the Finished Garment Measurements Chart deserves your attention. It will tell you whether a pattern adjustment is needed to get the correct length for your figure and for your fashion taste.

Tracing Your Pattern Pieces

One of the most important lessons you will learn in this first class is how to trace a *Stretch & Sew* pattern. I want you to be able to take full advantage of the many features of *Stretch & Sew* master patterns. You will use the measurements you have just taken to prepare a personal pattern to fit your figure. So I will take you through the procedure step by step. After you've done it once, you will find yourself tracing patterns in no time at all.

When you open up your pattern, you will find two sets of pattern pieces. Since you are sewing your first T-shirt from cotton single knit that has 25 percent stretch, work with the pattern pieces labelled "25% Stretch."

First you will trace the Front/Back. To do this, fold your pattern material and place the folded edge along the "Place on Fold" line of the Front/Back master pattern. In this way, you will end up with a whole pattern piece which will make it possible to cut your fabric for matching stripes. I suggest you use *Stretch & Sew*™ pattern weights to hold your pattern material in place as you trace.

When you trace your Front/Back, simply follow the outline of the pattern along the lines indicated for your size. For example, if your size is 36, trace along the lines labelled "36." If you are between sizes, draw between the lines for these sizes. You will draw in both the Front and Back necklines as illustrated.

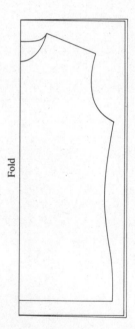

If your waist, hip, or back shoulder width varies from the measurement given for your size on the Standard Body Measurements Chart, you will need to make an adjustment *as you trace*. (Don't be concerned about a center back waist length adjustment at this time.) First find the size that your measurement does correspond to. If, for instance, you are a size 36 and your hips measure 40 inches (102.0 cm), you will find that your hip measurement falls under size 38. So, you will trace a size 36

for most of the pattern and a size 38 through the hips. Gradually taper from one size to the next as illustrated.

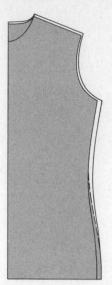

To give another example, suppose you are a size 36 and your back shoulder width is 15 inches (38.0 cm). After referring to the back of the pattern envelope, you will see that you are a size 34 through the shoulders. Gradually taper from size 36 to size 34 at the shoulders as illustrated. Notice that you keep your regular size along the shoulder edge. You only shift sizes along the armhole. When you trace your Sleeve, it will *not* be necessary to make a size adjustment.

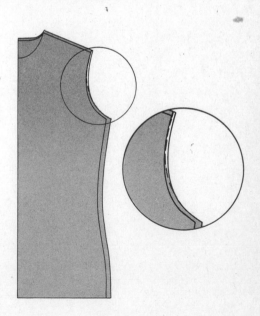

Some people find it necessary to combine more than two sizes to get a good fit. It's possible, for instance, to trace your size through the upper part of the pattern and go up or down a size at the waist and then up or down another size at the hips.

Now transfer all pattern markings to your pattern material and cut out your pattern piece. Label the Front/Back with the pattern name and number and add the size you have traced it in.

The next step is to compare your center back waist length measurement to the one given on the chart for your size. If they do not coincide, you will need to adjust the pattern so the garment waistline will match your body waistline.

To make this adjustment, cut the pattern on the shorten/lengthen line. If your measurement is smaller than the one on the chart, lap the pattern the difference between measurements and tape it in place. If your measurement is greater than the one on the chart, spread the pattern the difference between measurements and back the opening with pattern material.

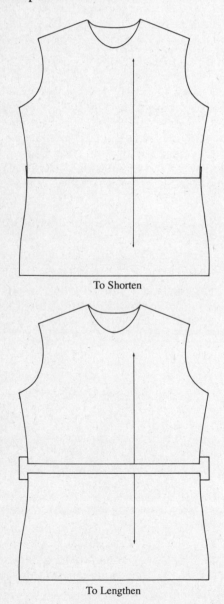

To Shorten

To Lengthen

In order to use the Front neckline, fold the Front/Back pattern piece in half. Starting at the shoulder neck edge, cut the neckline to a point ¼ inch (0.6 cm) short of the center front as illustrated. Then you will be able to fold down the Back neckline to cut a Front from your fabric.

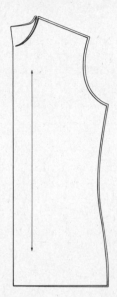

Next you will trace the Sleeve. Fold your pattern material and place the folded edge along the "Place on Fold" line of the Sleeve master pattern. Trace the outline of the pattern along the lines indicated for your size. Draw in the "Cutting Line for Short Sleeves" as illustrated.

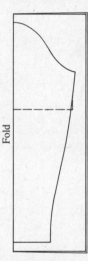

To cut short Sleeves, you will be able to fold the lower part of the pattern piece out of the way. To cut long Sleeves, fold the jog in the side of the pattern out of the way.

Now transfer all pattern markings to your pattern material and cut out your pattern piece. Label the Sleeve with the pattern name and number and add the size you have traced it in.

The next step is to compare your arm length measurement to the one given on the chart for your size. If they do not coincide, you will need to adjust the pattern.

To make this adjustment, cut the pattern on the shorten/lengthen line. If your measurement is smaller than the one on the chart, lap the pattern the difference between measurements and tape it in place. If your measurement is greater than the one on the chart, spread the pattern the difference between measurements and back the opening with pattern material.

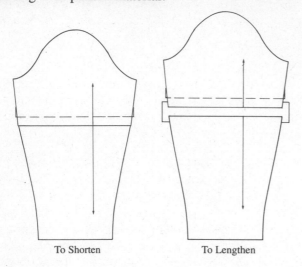

To Shorten   To Lengthen

Cutting Your Fabric

Pretreating

Pretreat the fabric you have selected for your T-shirt, following the care instructions which accompany the fabric. Remember to use soap or detergent in this first washing to remove any excess dye that could be on the fabric.

Do *not* pretreat ribbing unless you have selected a darker color such as red or navy trim to be used with a light-colored fabric. In this case, you would pretreat in order to remove any residual dye on the ribbing — but do it *after* cutting the trim to the correct length.

Cutting Garment Pieces

You will need to cut two Front/Backs, one to use as the Front and one to use as the Back. You will also need to cut two Sleeves — short or long. First cut open the fabric tube. To match stripes you must cut your pieces one at a time through a single thickness of fabric.

As you cut your fabric, make sure that the greater stretch in the fabric goes across the pattern pieces. Then the greater stretch will go around your body in the finished garment to provide you with a comfortable fit. The greater stretch in almost all knits runs across the fabric.

Another thing to keep in mind when working with single knits is that the folded edges of the fabric tube are permanent creases. It's important that you avoid the crease as you lay out most pattern pieces. An exception is cutting the Sleeves. You may place them on the fabric so the crease runs up and down along the exact center of each Sleeve. This is because most people press a crease along the centers of their sleeves anyway.

First cut one Front/Back. Make sure each underarm point is on the same stripe. You should also check to be sure the upper points of the pattern at the neck edge are on the same stripe as well as the points of the pattern at the upper armhole. Follow a stripe across the pattern lower edge.

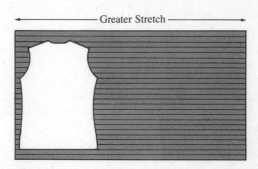

Use the first Front/Back you cut as a pattern for cutting the second Front/Back. Follow the same stripes between neck edges, upper armholes, underarm points, and at the lower edge. Then you will be able to match stripes when you sew the shoulder seams and the side seams. Take care not to stretch the garment piece as you handle it or your second Front/Back will be larger than it should be.

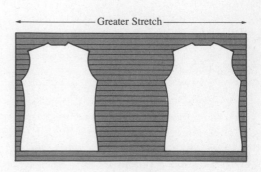

Fold down the Back neckline on the Front/Back pattern piece and place it on one Front/Back garment piece to cut the Front neckline. This garment piece will become your Front. The remaining piece will be the Back.

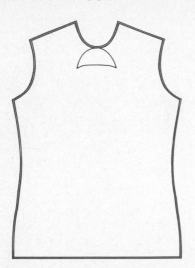

Now cut one Sleeve. Place the underarm points of the Sleeve on the same stripe you placed the underarm points of the Front/Back. You should also follow a stripe across the Sleeve lower edge. Then you will be able to match stripes when you sew the Sleeves to the T-shirt armholes and when you sew the Sleeve seams. Use the first Sleeve you cut as a pattern for cutting the second Sleeve, matching stripes exactly and taking care not to stretch the fabric.

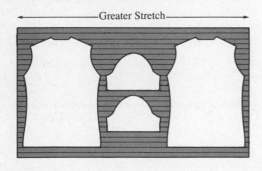
Greater Stretch

All that remains is cutting your ribbing for the trim, and you will do that during construction of the T-shirt.

Sewing Your T-Shirt

Sew your T-shirt seams with the right sides of the fabric together and with a ¼-inch (0.6 cm) seam allowance. Unless otherwise indicated, you should use a straight stitch with 9 stitches per inch (3 mm stitch length). Backstitch for reinforcement at the beginning and end of each seam.

Shoulder Seams

First you will sew the Front and Back together at the shoulders. When you stitch these seams, you will stretch the fabric as you sew. This is one of the techniques I developed when I was experimenting with knit fabrics.

An old-fashioned idea about sewing with knits was that all seams should be stabilized, but that contradicts my attitude that the seams must have elasticity to hang attractively. Also, if the seams are able to give when you move your body or when you are pulling the garment on and off, the threads will resist breaking and you will have stronger seams.

The important thing to keep in mind when sewing any knit garment is that the seams must have the same elasticity as the fabric itself. You should be certain that you stretch the seam as much as the fabric wants to stretch easily.

Another thing I learned as I developed this technique was that it works best with a longer straight stitch. A zigzag stitch or a short straight stitch puts too much thread in a seam and may cause it to ruffle. That's why I recommend that you sew the seams in your garments with a straight stitch, using 9 stitches per inch (3 mm stitch length). When the seam relaxes into its normal shape, the stitches will appear shorter but they will expand again when stress is applied to the seam.

With that explanation, you are ready to begin sewing. Pin the shoulder seams with the right sides of the fabric together, taking care to match stripes.

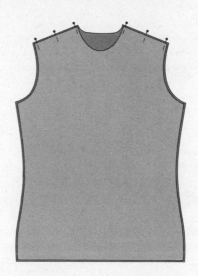

Then stitch each seam ¼ inch (0.6 cm) from the shoulder edges, starting at the armhole and sewing toward the neckline. As you sew, hold the fabric behind the presser foot with one hand, and in front, hold it with your other hand, stretching as much as the fabric wants to give easily.

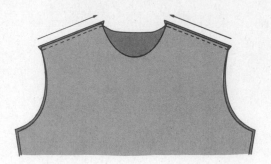

It's a good idea to check now — before you sew the cross seams — to determine whether you've stretched enough. Pull on the seams as much as the fabric wants to give easily. If any threads break, restitch, stretching more firmly as you sew.

To add strength to the seams and to prevent the seam allowances from rolling when you are sewing with single knit, doublestitch. To doublestitch, sew a second line of stitching *on the seam allowance* ⅛ inch (0.3 cm) from the previous stitching. Again, you should stretch as you sew.

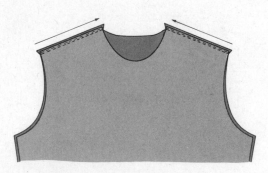

This is the time to begin developing the habit of pressing seams immediately after sewing them for a professional-looking finished garment. Press the shoulder seam allowances toward the Back of the T-shirt.

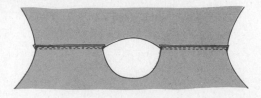

Crew Neckband

Applying the crew neckband is one of the most exciting techniques you will learn in your class series. The first step is trimming the neck edge of the T-shirt ¾ inch (1.9 cm). This fabric must be removed to make room for the crew neckband which should come only to the natural neckline on the body.

To trim the garment neck edge, fold it in half as illustrated. Then trim through a double thickness of fabric ¾ inch (1.9 cm) all the way around. If you don't trust your eye, use a *Stretch & Sew*™ fabric marker to draw in a cutting line.

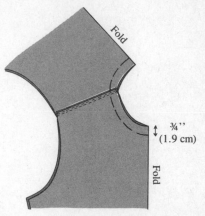

The length of your ribbing strip must be two-thirds the length of the garment neck edge with ½ inch (1.3 cm) added for seam allowance. This means you will be applying the trim to the neck edge with a 2:3 ratio — 2 inches (5.1 cm) of ribbing to 3 inches (7.6 cm) of neck edge. As you sew, you will be able to stretch the ribbing to match the garment neck edge. Afterwards, the ribbing will relax to its normal length at the natural neckline, providing a close-fitting crew neckband.

While the garment is folded, measure the neck edge of your T-shirt, standing the tape on its side for accuracy. Double this amount to determine the total neck edge measurement.

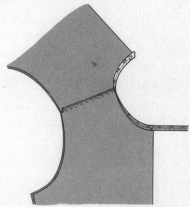

A handy way to determine two-thirds of the neck edge is to fold the length of the measurement on the tape into thirds. If, for instance, the measurement was 21 inches (53.3 cm), fold the first 21 inches (53.3 cm) of the tape as illustrated.

Then unfold the last third and read the tape at the end of the second third. For our example of a 21-inch (53.3 cm) neck edge, you will have a reading of 14 inches (35.6 cm). Add ½ inch (1.3 cm) for seam allowance.

Another way to determine two-thirds of the neck edge measurement is to divide the measurement by 3, and then, multiply your answer by 2. For our example of a 21-inch (53.3 cm) neck edge, divide 21 by 3 to get 7. Then multiply 2 times 7 to get 14 inches. Add ½ inch (1.3 cm) for seam allowance.

$$\overset{\displaystyle 7}{3\,\big/\,21}$$

$$2 \times 7 = 14$$

$$14 + \tfrac{1}{2} = 14\tfrac{1}{2}$$

Open the tube of ribbing and cut a strip 2½ inches (6.4 cm) wide by the two-thirds measurement plus ½ inch (1.3 cm). The greater stretch of the ribbing should run the length of the strip.

Greater Stretch

Now sew the ends of the ribbing together with a ¼-inch (0.6 cm) seam allowance, forming a circle. Finger-press the seam allowances open.

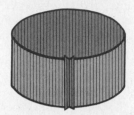

With wrong sides together, fold the circle of ribbing in half as illustrated.

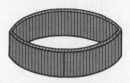

Because the circle of ribbing is smaller around than the neck edge of the T-shirt, you must stretch the ribbing to fit as you sew it in place. To help you stretch evenly, you will divide the circle of ribbing and the neck edge into fourths, marking the divisions with pins. To divide the ribbing in fourths, place one pin at the seam and a second pin directly across from the seam as illustrated.

Then refold the circle, matching pins, and place a third and fourth pin at the quarter divisions.

To divide the neck edge of the T-shirt into fourths, place one pin at the center back and a second pin at the center front as illustrated.

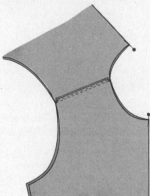

Then refold the T-shirt, matching pins, and place a third and fourth pin at the quarter divisions.

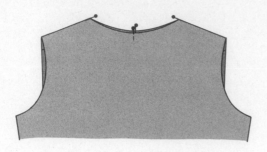

As you can see, the shoulder seams are *not* quarter divisions.

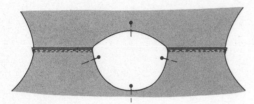

Placing the seam of the ribbing at the center back, pin the ribbing to the T-shirt as illustrated, matching quarter divisions.

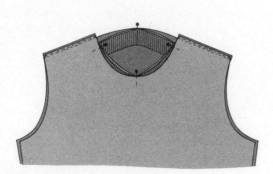

Now, with the ribbing on top and the T-shirt next to the sewing machine, start stitching at the center back, using a ¼-inch (0.6 cm) seam allowance. Stretch the ribbing between quarter divisions to match the neck opening. It's not necessary to stretch the neck edge of the T-shirt. Make certain that the T-shirt is smooth underneath and that you keep the three cut layers of fabric together as you sew around the circle.

Remove the T-shirt from the sewing machine and turn the garment to its finished position to see the wonderful crew neckband you have just created.

Press the seam allowances toward the inside of the garment. Touch the iron to the seam allowances only in order to avoid creasing the fold in the neckband or pressing the ribbing out of shape.

One step remains to complete the crew neckband and that is to stitch the neckline a second time by topstitching. This will keep the seam allowances in place so your neckband will stay new-looking.

Topstitch the T-shirt ⅛ inch (0.3 cm) from the neckline seam, catching the seam allowances on the underside and stretching slightly as you sew. When you topstitch, sew on the right side of the garment with 6 stitches per inch (4 mm stitch length). This larger stitch length creates distinctive stitches for an attractive finish and it prevents a ruffled appearance which may occur from too much thread along the seam.

Sleeves

Now you've arrived at another exciting technique — stretching in the Sleeves. You'll find it amazingly simple and you'll be thrilled at being able to match stripes with the body of the T-shirt.

First, fold the Sleeve in half and mark the center of the Sleeve cap with a pin.

Place the Sleeve right sides together with the armhole, pinning the center of the Sleeve cap to the shoulder seam. Pin the Sleeve to the T-shirt at the underarm points and pin again halfway between the underarm and the center of the Sleeve cap. You will be able to match stripes to the halfway point. However, it isn't possible to match them through the Sleeve cap.

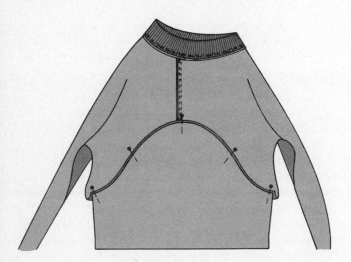

You will sew the armhole seam with the T-shirt on top and the Sleeve next to the sewing machine, stretching the armhole to fit the Sleeve. Once when I was teaching a class, a woman said to me, "Now, Ann, you have the garment on top and the Sleeve on the bottom, and the garment is being stretched while the Sleeve is relaxed. Does that mean you sew with a *relaxed bottom*?"

I said, "Yes, that's exactly what I'm telling you to do." And this is a principle to remember in all your knit sewing. You practiced it as you applied your crew neckband though you may not have thought of it in this way.

So, stitch the armhole seam as I've described, using a ¼-inch (0.6 cm) seam allowance and stretching the armhole to match the Sleeve. Take care to match stripes between the underarms and the beginning of the Sleeve cap. Then doublestitch the armhole seam.

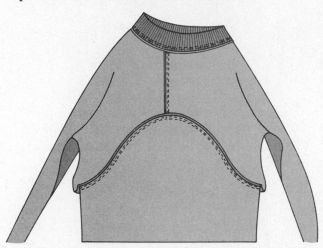

Stretch in the second Sleeve in the same manner as the first. Press the seam allowances toward the Sleeves.

Side Seams

Now pin the side seams from the lower edge of the T-shirt through the underarms to the lower edge of the Sleeves. As you sew your first T-shirt, careful pinning will help you to match stripes.

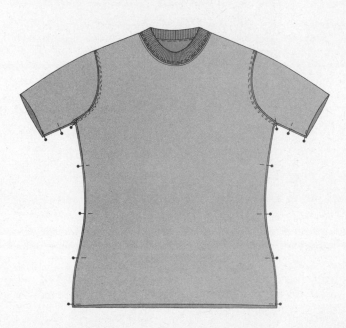

Stitch each side seam, starting at the garment lower edge and stretching as you sew. Doublestitch these seams.

Press the seam allowances toward the Back of the T-shirt.

Hems

Only one step remains and that's putting in the hems. For your T-shirt, I want to teach you the principles of applying machine-stitched hems. Machine-stitched hems suit the sporty look of the T-shirt and they have the advantage of being extra quick and easy.

First press in a 1-inch (2.5 cm) hem at the lower edge of each Sleeve and a 1½-inch (3.8 cm) hem at the lower edge of the T-shirt. Pin the hems in place so the heads of the pins extend beyond the folded edges for easy removal as you stitch.

When you sew in the hem, start at the side seam and stitch on the right side of the T-shirt. This may be something new for you, but it's a wonderful way to apply a hem. You'll find that the garment itself holds the hem in place as you're sewing along. You will be able to feel the cut edge through the fabric with your fingertips to be sure you're catching the hem allowance in your stitching. For the Sleeve hems, you should stitch approximately ¾ inch (1.9 cm) from the folded edge. At the garment lower edge, stitch approximately 1¼ inches (3.2 cm) from the folded edge.

If you're using a straight stitch, stretch slightly as you sew to build strength into the hem. You don't want the stitches to pop as you pull the T-shirt on and off. When

you are sewing with striped fabric, you may use a straight stitch for a nearly invisible hem. Select thread that matches one of the stripes and, then, sew along the edge of the stripe, stitching on the right side of the garment.

Another stitch I enjoy using for hems is a zigzag stitch. This stitch provides its own stretch so you don't need to stretch while you sew. In fact, you should *not* stretch with a zigzag stitch because this would build too much thread into the hem and cause a ruffled hemline.

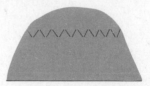

There are many decorative stitches you may use for hems when you are sewing on solid-colored fabric. One stitch is the multiple zigzag stitch — a series of small stitches in a zigzag pattern.

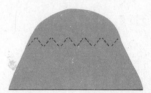

I'll mention one more machine-stitched hem which is a real favorite of mine — a hem topstitched with a double needle. To use a double needle, you will need a zigzag sewing machine. This needle sews a double row of straight stitches on the surface of the garment. The double row of stitches is perfectly spaced with no extra care on your part. A tiny ridge of fabric, which looks like a small tuck, is created between the rows, and a zigzag stitch is created on the wrong side to build stretch into the stitching.

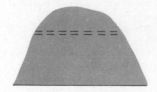 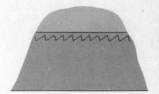

So, select your stitch and complete your T-shirt by sewing in the hem. Not only have you sewn yourself a wonderful garment, but you've learned many of the skills for sewing more garments to come.

Special Information

Figuring a 3:4 Ratio

When you applied the crew neckband to the T-shirt, you learned how to determine a 2:3 ratio. In your sewing, you will sometimes apply trim with a 3:4 ratio — 3 inches (7.6 cm) of trim to 4 inches (10.2 cm) of garment edge. To do this, you will need to determine three-fourths of the garment edge measurement.

One way is to fold the length of the measurement on the tape into fourths. Then unfold the last fourth and read the tape at the end of the third fourth. Another way is to divide the measurement by 4, and then, multiply your answer by 3.

Options for the Second Stitching of the Neckline

When you sewed your T-shirt for Class 1, you learned to topstitch the neckline, which provides a second row of stitching to strengthen the seam and stabilize the seam allowances. There are several other ways this can be accomplished, creating different finished appearances in the garment.

One method is to simply doublestitch the neckline by sewing a second row of stitching on the seam allowances ⅛ inch (0.3 cm) from the previous stitching. With this method, the second row of stitching does not show from the right side of the T-shirt, giving the garment a less sporty look.

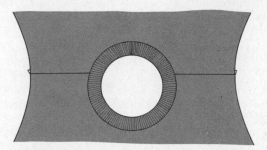

Another method is to doublestitch only the Front neckline by sewing a second row of stitching on the seam allowances ⅛ inch (0.3 cm) from the previous stitching. Then topstitch the Back ⅛ inch (0.3 cm) from the shoulder and neck seams as illustrated. For this top-stitching, stretch slightly as you sew, using 6 stitches per inch (4 mm stitch length). This method gives the garment a very sporty look which is often seen in men's and children's T-shirts.

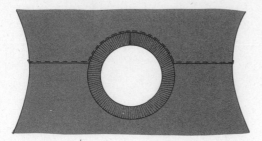

T-Shirt from Cotton Interlock

Another fabric that is ideal for T-shirts is cotton interlock. This fabric has slightly more weight than cotton single knit and it is more elastic, having approximately 50 percent stretch. It appears nearly the same on both sides of the fabric and the cut edges do not curl. Cotton interlock is similar to cotton single knit in that it is knit in a tube and the folded edges are permanent creases.

What you will truly enjoy in this fabric is its soft, soft surface and its gentle hand. It's perfect for children's T-shirts as well as your own. And it comes in a broad range of fashion colors coordinated with other *Stretch & Sew* fabrics.

To make your T-shirt from cotton interlock, all you have to do is trace the pieces from the T-Shirts Pattern No. 310 which are labelled "50% Stretch." The construction techniques are the same. You may wish to sew your second T-shirt from cotton interlock with a turtleneck finish as described in the following instructions.

The Turtleneck T-Shirt

A turtleneck finish gives the T-shirt another look, creating a knit top that goes great with skirts, jumpers or pantsuits.

For your turtleneck T-shirt refer to the back of the T-Shirts Pattern No. 310 for yardage and notions. You will find that 12 inches (30.5 cm) of ribbing is required for the turtleneck trim.

Prepare your pattern, cut your fabric, and sew the shoulder seams as described earlier in this chapter for the T-shirt with a crew neckband.

Turtleneck Application

When you apply a turtleneck, you *do not* trim the neckline of the T-shirt as you would for a crew neckband. This is because a turtleneck should start at your natural neckline and come up around your neck.

You will be applying the turtleneck trim with a 1:1 ratio — 1 inch (2.5 cm) of ribbing to 1 inch (2.5 cm) of neck edge. To determine the length for the ribbing strip, measure the neck edge of the T-shirt and add ½ inch (1.3 cm) for seam allowance. Cut a strip of ribbing this length by 12 inches (30.5 cm) wide. The greater stretch of the ribbing should run the length of the strip.

Sew the ends of the ribbing together with ¼-inch (0.6 cm) seam allowance, forming a circle. Finger-press the seam allowance open.

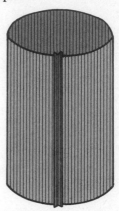

With wrong sides together, fold the circle of ribbing in half. Then divide the circle in fourths, marking the divisions with pins.

Next divide the neck edge of the T-shirt into fourths, marking the divisions with pins. As you can see, the shoulder seams are *not* quarter divisions.

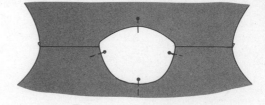

Placing the seam of the ribbing at the center back, pin the ribbing to the T-shirt as illustrated, matching quarter divisions.

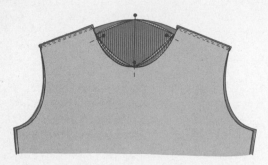

Now, with the ribbing on top and the T-shirt next to the sewing machine, start stitching at the center back, using a ¼-inch (0.6 cm) seam allowance. Stretch the ribbing *and* the garment neck edge as you sew. It's necessary to stretch the garment neck edge because the seam will be stretched when you pull the turtleneck over your head.

Doublestitch the neckline seam. Press the seam allowances to the inside of the garment, touching the iron to the seam allowances only. Next, fold the turtleneck to its finished position and continue with construction. Stretch in the Sleeves, sew the side seams, and hem the T-shirt as described earlier in this chapter.

Zipper in a Shoulder Seam

Applying a zipper in the shoulder seam of a T-shirt is simple to do and it's particularly useful for children's T-shirts because children have proportionately large heads. With a zipper, their T-shirts can have a close-fitting crew neckband that's not difficult to pull on and off. For this technique I recommend a nylon coil zipper rather than one with metal teeth.

Prepare the pattern and cut your fabric as described earlier in this chapter for your T-shirt.

Shoulder Seam and Crew Neckband

Sew the *right* shoulder seam only. By "right," I'm referring to the finished garment as if you were wearing it. Doublestitch this seam.

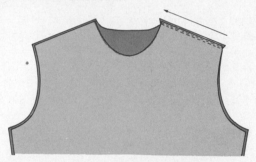

Press the seam allowances toward the Back of the T-shirt. Then trim the neck edge ¾ inch (1.9 cm) all the way around.

Next measure the neck edge of the T-shirt and cut a strip of ribbing two-thirds of this measurement by 2½ inches (6.4 cm) wide. The greater stretch of the ribbing should run the length of the strip. Fold the ribbing in half lengthwise and divide the strip into fourths as illustrated.

Divide the neck edge of the T-shirt into fourths, using the left shoulder as one of the quarter divisions. The center front and center back are *not* quarter divisions.

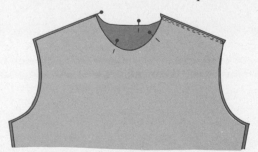

Pin the ribbing to the neck edge with right sides together, matching quarter divisions. With the ribbing on top and the T-shirt next to the sewing machine, stitch with a ¼-inch (0.6 cm) seam allowance, stretching the ribbing to match the neck opening.

Press the seam allowances to the inside of the garment, touching the iron to the seam allowances only. With 6 stitches per inch (4 mm stitch length), topstitch the T-shirt ⅛ inch (0.3 cm) from the neckline seam, catching the seam allowances on the underside and stretching slightly as you sew.

Zipper Application

Place one side of the zipper face down on the right side of the Front. Position the edge of the zipper tape even with the shoulder edge and the zipper pull at the fold of the crew neckband. The zipper may extend past the armhole. Pin the zipper in place. Then, using a zipper foot, sew along the tape next to the zipper teeth.

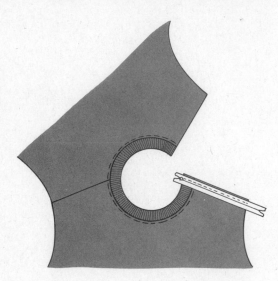

Place the second side of the zipper face down on the right side of the Back. Again, position the edge of the zipper tape even with the shoulder edge and the zipper pull at the fold of the crew neckband. Using a zipper foot, sew along the tape next to the zipper teeth.

Unzip the zipper. Then fold the ends of the zipper tape at the neck edge to the wrong side of the T-shirt.

Next fold the zipper to its finished position and pin as illustrated. The ends of the zipper tape will be concealed between the zipper and the ribbing.

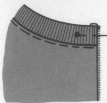

Either hand stitch the ends of the zipper tape in place or secure them by topstitching on either side of the zipper ⅛ inch (0.3 cm) from the zipper teeth as illustrated.

Now you will stretch in the Sleeves as described in the earlier part of the chapter, sewing over the closed zipper as if it were an ordinary shoulder seam. After you have completed the armhole seams, cut off any excess zipper. The doublestitching in the armhole seam will keep the zipper together. Sew the side seams and stitch the hems to complete the T-shirt.

Chapter 2
Women's Pants and Four-Gore Skirt

Introduction

At last a pattern for pants that fit! I have often thought that all designers of commercial pants patterns must believe all women are amazons. For me pants patterns were designed with a crotch that hit below the knee. And once a crotch is cut too deep, there is no way to shorten it. So one of my first objectives in my early days of pattern-making was designing a pants pattern to fit a woman's figure.

Pattern No. 700 has been our top-selling pattern since the first days of Stretch & Sew. So, our customers have communicated to us that they like the fit of our pants pattern. At Stretch & Sew we don't follow the set rules of the past. We make our own rules — based on the needs of thousands of women we have met in the years that have gone by since my first pattern on butcher paper in 1967.

When you visit your *Stretch & Sew Fabrics*® center, you will find pants already sewn in each size. You will be able to try them on to determine your correct size and receive help in fitting your figure. Imagine what a boon this has been to our customers!

In Class 2 you will learn to sew pants and you will also learn to sew a four-gore skirt that features the same turned-down elastic finish. This is one of the easy techniques you will discover again and again in *Stretch & Sew*® patterns to really cut down on your sewing time.

Equally exciting are the Stretch & Sew products you will discover in Class 2. Your teacher will introduce you to a perfect fabric for your pants, skirts, and jackets — a fabric that comes in a rainbow of fashion colors coordinated with other *Stretch & Sew*® fabrics.

For the turned-down elastic waist finish, you will be using *Stretch & Sew*™ braided elastic which is wonderful for strength. It just doesn't wear out. And, you will learn how to apply *Perky Bond*® fusible web in hems to save you hours and hours of time in your sewing.

70%

Women's Pants and Four-Gore Skirt

Pattern Selection

Stretch & Sew Pattern No. 700

The pants you will be making in Class 2 are from *Stretch & Sew* Pattern No. 700. Like all *Stretch & Sew* pants patterns, Pattern No. 700 has a line for adjusting "crotch depth." You'll learn how to make this simple adjustment during Class 2.

Pattern No. 700 also features a shorts line. So you will be able to create your own pattern for shorts that will be the mainstay of your summer and active sportswear wardrobe. The shorts sew up with the same simple construction techniques as for the pants.

Stretch & Sew Pattern No. 430

The four-gore skirt you are sewing for Class 2 is View A of *Stretch & Sew* Pattern No. 430. This pattern offers three other skirt styles. View B is a multi-gore skirt with narrow gores that are creased and topstitched for a pleated look. View C features an inverted center front pleat, and View D is a flared skirt.

The four-gore skirt has four skirt panels — all cut from one pattern piece — which sew up to form an A-line silhouette. In class you will learn to make the skirt with the quick and easy turned-down elastic waist finish I mentioned before.

Fabric Selection

Fabric for Your Pants

Stretch & Sew Pattern No. 700 is designed to be used with fabric that has 25 percent horizontal stretch. Because the stretch in the fabric provides ease in the pants, it's important that you select a fabric which has the correct amount of stretch. If the fabric has much less than 25 percent stretch, your pants will be too tight. If the fabric has much more stretch, your pants will be too loose.

The method for determining the percentage of stretch is simple. Fold your fabric approximately 12 inches (30.5 cm) from one cut edge.

Place 10 inches (25.4 cm) of the fold along the first 10 inches (25.4 cm) of your tape measure.

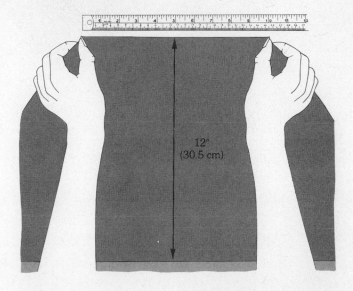

Hold the fabric in place at the left end of the tape. With your right hand, pull the fold past the 10-inch (25.4 cm) mark as far as it will comfortably go. If the fabric will stretch *easily* to 12½ inches (31.8 cm), you have 25 percent stretch. If it stretches to only 11 inches (27.9 cm), you have less than 25 percent stretch. If it stretches to 15 inches (38.1 cm), you have 50 percent stretch.

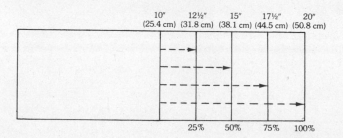

An important question is how far will it stretch under medium tension? Don't stretch with all your might. There should be some stretch left in the fabric. If I can stretch a piece of fabric easily to show 25 percent stretch, I can usually force it to show 35 percent.

Most knit fabrics have approximately 25 percent stretch. So you will have a wide choice from which to make a selection. Your *Stretch & Sew Fabrics* center carries fabrics especially designed to be used for your pants. Your teacher will help you select the perfect fabric for you.

You will find that many of the most popular fabrics for pants are polyester double knit. Polyester is a durable fiber, creating a fabric that holds its shape and resists wrinkles to keep your pants good-looking with no trouble to you. And, when pressed correctly, polyester holds a wonderful crease that will last through many washings. *Stretch & Sew* polyester fabrics are made from brand name fibers. As a double check, we conduct quality control tests to ensure you of the highest possible performance in our fabrics.

Double knit provides the perfect weight for pants. Many types of stitches are used in the knitting process, creating a great variety in double knit fabrics. You may select from smooth solids, plaids, nubby tweeds, soft flannels, and corduroys. There's no end to what you'll find, depending on the fashion trends.

And, of course, *Stretch & Sew* double knit polyesters are color-coordinated with our other fabrics. Your teacher will help you select fabric for your pants to build a wardrobe. You can mix and match your pants with everything else you sew to have more outfits from fewer garments.

Fabric for Your Four-Gore Skirt

The four-gore skirt is attractive in a wide variety of fabrics. Make it up in a mediumweight fabric for fall and winter. Or try a lightweight fabric for spring and summer.

An idea for you to consider is sewing your first skirt in fabric to match your pants. Then when you come to Class 7, make your jacket from *Stretch & Sew* Pattern No. 1040 using the same fabric, and you'll have a three-piece suit! If you decide that this is the direction you want to take, buy your fabric now. It's best to buy all your fabric from one bolt because it will be from the same dye lot. Approximately five yards (4.57 m) is a good amount of fabric to purchase for your suit.

Yardage and Notions

After you have selected your fabric, refer to the back of the pattern envelope for yardage and notions. Pattern No. 700 and Pattern No. 430 both require *Stretch & Sew* ¾-inch (1.9 cm) elastic. This is a braided elastic which provides the precise degree of stretch necessary for the turned-down elastic waist finish. And it is designed to hold its strength even when you stitch through it.

Women's Pants

Preparing Your Pattern

Determining Your Pattern Size

You will trace the pattern pieces for your pants according to your hip size. Take your hip measurement 9 inches (22.9 cm) below the waist, measuring over undergarments you will wear with the pants. To be sure you are measuring from the natural waistline, tie a strip of elastic around your middle. The lower edge of the elastic will "find" the narrowest part of your waist.

Your hip measurement determines your hip size. Hold the tape so it's snug against your hips but not tight. You should be able to feel the tape against your body, yet it should be loose enough to slide back and forth. Don't fudge when you read the tape. A white lie now will make you unhappy when you do your final fitting.

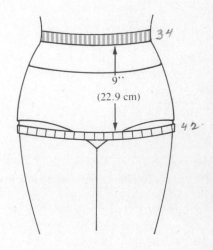

Next, take your waist measurement, holding the tape so that it's snug against the waist but not tight.

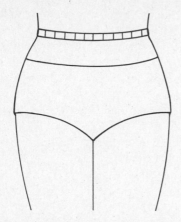

So many women end up wearing pants that pull through the crotch even though they may fit in the waist and hips. Or the pants are terribly baggy because they are too long in the crotch. To be sure this doesn't happen to you, take a crotch depth or ''sit'' measurement.

To take your sit measurement, tie elastic around your waist. Then, sit on a table with the bend in your knees against the table edge. I recommend a table because a firm, flat surface is necessary for an accurate sit measurement. A desk or kitchen counter will do as well. Sit up straight and measure from the lower edge of the elastic at your waist, over the curve of your hip, straight down to the table.

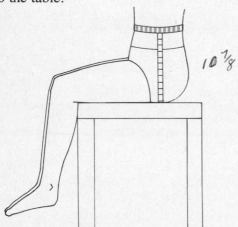

Write down your sit measurement. You will adjust your pattern, if necessary, after it has been traced.

Referring to the Standard Body Measurements Chart on the back of the pattern envelope, choose the size that corresponds to your hip measurement. Compare your body waist measurement to the waist measurement for your size. If your waist measurement is larger than the one given for your size, you will need to trace your pattern in a larger size at the waist.

If your waist measurement is smaller than the one given for your size, you may trace the pattern one size smaller at the waist. Remember, however, that the pants must pull up over the hips. It's best not to trace down more than one size. Instead, rely on the elastic to draw in the waistline of your pants.

I feel that the easiest and surest way to determine pant length is to measure a pair you already have. Choose a pair that is a good length with the shoes you'll be wearing with your new pants, and measure the inseam. Compare this measurement to the inseam length listed under the Finished Garment Measurements Chart on the back of the pattern envelope and determine whether you need to shorten or lengthen the pattern pieces when you trace them.

Tracing Your Pattern Pieces

Trace one Front and one Back in your hip size. If you are tracing up or down in size at the waist, do not make an adjustment at the center front and center back because you need to maintain the smooth crotch line of the pattern. To compensate for not adjusting at the center front and center back, trace up or down *two* sizes along the sides to create *one* size difference in the waistline. Trace the pattern upper edge in your regular hip size.

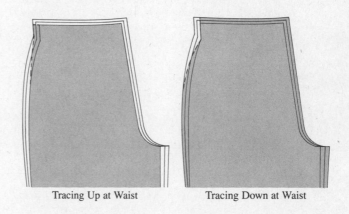

Tracing Up at Waist   Tracing Down at Waist

Shorten or lengthen the pants, if necessary, at the pattern lower edge as you do your tracing.

Transfer all pattern markings to your tracing material. I also like to note the fabric I'm using, the size and length I'm tracing, and the date. Then, after a period of time, it's easy to remember whether to trace a new pattern to account for a gain or loss in weight or whether I need to adjust length because of fashion or for a different shoe style.

Adjusting Crotch Depth

Compare your sit measurement to the crotch depth given for your size on the chart below:

Size	Crotch Depth (Sit Measurement)
30	9 inches (22.9 cm)
32	9¼ inches (23.5 cm)
34	9½ inches (24.1 cm)
36	9¾ inches (24.8 cm)
38	10 inches (25.4 cm)
40	10¼ inches (26.0 cm)
42	10½ inches (26.7 cm)
44	10¾ inches (27.3 cm)
46	11 inches (27.9 cm)

If the measurements are not the same, you must make an adjustment on both the Front and Back pattern pieces. Cut on the lines for adjusting crotch depth and add or subtract the difference between measurements.

For example, if the sit measurement corresponding to your size is 10 inches (25.4 cm), and your own sit measurement is 9 inches (22.9 cm), subtract 1 inch (2.5 cm) from both the Front and the Back.

To do this, cut on the shorten/lengthen lines and lap each pattern piece 1 inch (2.5 cm), keeping the straight-of-grain line matched. Tape the lapped pattern in place.

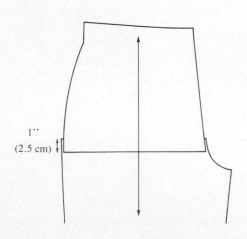

1"
(2.5 cm)

Or, if the sit measurement corresponding to your size is 10 inches (25.4 cm), and your own sit measurement is 11 inches (27.9 cm), add 1 inch (2.5 cm) to both the Front and the Back.

To do this, cut on the shorten/lengthen lines and back the opening with pattern material. Spread the opening exactly 1 inch (2.5 cm), keeping the straight-of-grain aligned. Tape the paper in place and use your fashion ruler to connect the lines on the pattern.

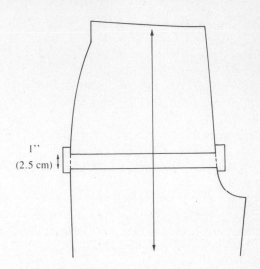

1"
(2.5 cm)

You are well on your way to having a pair of pants that fits your figure. What an accomplishment! For most of you, the pattern you have just traced will provide a wonderful fit. If, after sewing your first pair of pants, you find that the fit could be improved, refer to *The Stretch & Sew® Pants Book,* an excellent source of pant-fitting information for special figure types.

Cutting Your Fabric

Pretreating

As usual, you will want to pretreat the fabric you have selected for your pants. Do not pretreat the elastic.

Cutting Garment Pieces

From your fabric, cut two Fronts and two Backs, referring to the Suggested Cutting Layouts in the pattern instructions. If your fabric doesn't have a distinctive right and wrong side, mark a right side for each piece as you cut it, using a pin or a strip of self-adhesive basting tape. For plaid fabric, refer to "Special Information" at the end of the chapter.

Remember to place the pattern pieces on the fabric so the greater stretch will go around the body in the finished garment. Whenever you're cutting through a single thickness of fabric, cut one piece and then turn the pattern over to cut the second piece. In this way, you will always be sure to have both a right side and left side for your garment.

You will also need to cut a strip of *Stretch & Sew* ¾-inch (1.9 cm) elastic 2 inches (5.1 cm) less than your body waist measurement.

Sewing Your Pants

Sew your pants right sides together with the ⅝-inch (1.6 cm) seam allowance indicated on the pattern. Unless otherwise indicated, you should use a straight stitch with 9 stitches per inch (3 mm stitch length) and stretch as you sew. As usual, I recommend that you backstitch at the beginning and end of each seam.

Side Seams

If your pant legs are to fall straight without twisting, you must take care to stretch each layer of fabric the same amount as you stitch your seams. Careful pinning will help you stretch the fabric evenly. Place a Front and Back in a relaxed position on a flat surface and pin the side seam, placing a pin approximately every 8 inches (20.3 cm).

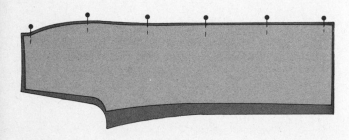

Stitch the side seam, beginning at the lower edge and stretching both layers of fabric evenly as you sew. You will start stitching each seam in your pants at the lower edge. This directional stitching ensures that the pant legs will fall straight while you wear the finished garment.

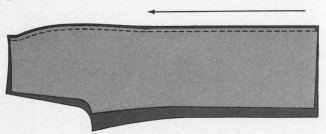

Pin the second pant leg and stitch the side seam in the same manner, beginning at the lower edge.

Place each pant leg on the ironing board and press the outside leg seam open, using a damp press cloth and a steam iron (wool setting). Hold the iron firmly in one place until the press cloth is dry. Repeat until the entire

seam has been pressed open. Remember to allow the fabric to cool before you move the pant leg from the ironing board.

This careful pressing will provide a professional finish to your pants which will last through many, many launderings. For success in your sewing, develop a habit of pressing as you sew. Every time you sew a seam, imagine that I am there telling you to get up and press that seam.

Inside Leg Seams

Pin and stitch each inside leg seam, beginning at the lower edge and stretching both layers of fabric evenly as you sew.

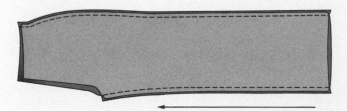

Carefully press the seams open, using a damp cloth and a steam iron.

Creases at Midconstruction

Sharp, straight creases create a finished look to your pants, and they are slimming as well. Polyester and wool may be permanently creased. This is a great convenience but you must take care when you press in the creases — for you'll live with the result for a long while. Each crease should fall exactly halfway between the inside and outside leg seams.

This is a convenient time to crease your pants so I'll tell you how to do it at this point in construction. However, if you're sewing your first pair, I recommend you wait until you have tried on the pants to check the fit. I'll be discussing creases again later in the chapter for those of you who wait.

To press creases now, turn the pant legs right side out. Place a pant leg on the ironing board and match the inside leg seam to the outside leg seam, following the straight-of-grain up the center front and center back of the pant leg. There will be a little extra fullness at the upper inside leg seam.

Use a steam iron (wool setting) and a damp press cloth. Hold the iron firmly in one place until the press cloth is dry. Repeat until you have pressed a crease in the front from the bottom of the leg up to the waist. In back, crease the pants from the bottom of the leg to crotch level. Crease the second pant leg in the same manner.

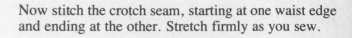

Back Crease

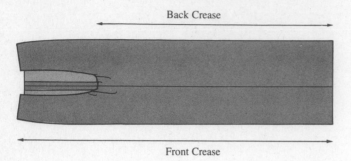

Front Crease

Crotch Seam

Next you will sew the crotch seam. Turn one leg wrong side out. Then, place the other leg inside it so that the right sides of the legs face each other. Matching the inside leg seams and the waist edges, pin the crotch seam.

Because this is a stress seam, you must stretch very firmly as you stitch it, especially through the lower crotch curve. To help you maintain an exact ⅝-inch (1.6 cm) seam allowance, you may wish to mark the seamline of the lower crotch curve before you sew it. I suggest you use a *Stretch & Sew*™ fabric marker for this purpose.

Now stitch the crotch seam, starting at one waist edge and ending at the other. Stretch firmly as you sew.

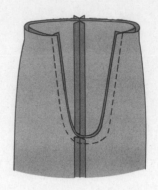

If you marked the seamline with a *Stretch & Sew* fabric marker, take a moment now to remove the ink, using a cloth thoroughly moistened with tap water. Do not wait until after laundering the pants.

For reinforcement, I recommend you doublestitch the lower crotch curve. First, mark it with pins, following the illustration.

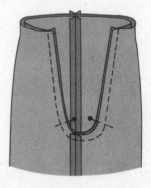

Then stitch close to the previous stitching between the pins, stretching as you sew.

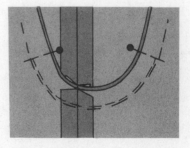

For a smooth and comfortable fit, it's necessary to trim the lower crotch curve. If you are sewing your pants from light-colored fabric, take care that you don't trim too high or the tapered seam allowance may be noticeable from the right side. Trim by tapering from ⅝ inch (1.6 cm) to ¼ inch (0.6 cm) along the doublestitched portion of the seam.

Press the untrimmed portions of the crotch seam open, taking the same care as when you pressed the leg seams.

Turned-Down Elastic Waist

The turned-down elastic finish is one of the central sewing techniques you will learn in your classes. You are using it now for your pants, but it is also used in skirts, swimsuits, and body suits.

If you have not already cut your elastic, cut a strip of *Stretch & Sew* ¾-inch (1.9 cm) elastic 2 inches (5.1 cm) less than your body waist measurement. Lap the ends of the elastic ½ inch (1.3 cm), forming a circle, and stitch them together securely.

Now divide the elastic in fourths and mark the divisions with pins — just as you divided the cylinder of ribbing for the crew neck on your T-shirt. However, avoid using the lapped seam as one of your quarter divisions.

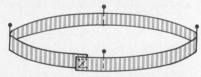

Pin the elastic to the wrong side of the pants even with the upper edge, matching the quarter divisions to the four seams of the pants.

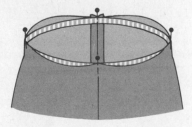

With the elastic on top and the pants next to the sewing machine, zigzag the elastic to the pants along the upper edge, stretching the elastic to fit the waist. Or you may use a straight stitch, but you must stretch *both* thicknesses as you sew.

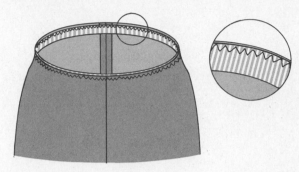

If you would like a handy way to mark the back of your pants, take a moment to cut a strip of fabric approximately ½ inch (1.3 cm) wide by 2½ inches (6.4 cm) long. Fold the strip in half and pin it in place at the center back waist edge as illustrated.

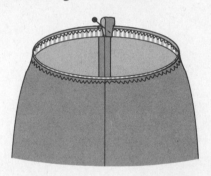

When you fold down the elastic for finishing, the loop will turn to the inside of the pants, marking the back. Another easy way to mark the back is to sew in a *Stretch & Sew*™ garment label after you complete the pants. Either way, you won't have to give the pants a second look when you're getting yourself together on a busy morning.

Fold the elastic to the wrong side of the pants and pin it in place. Keep the fabric pulled straight and taut with the edge of the elastic right against the fold of the fabric.

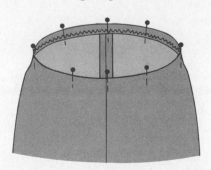

Zigzag the waistline again. This time the zigzag stitch should just overlap the lower edge of the elastic as illustrated. Stretch as you sew and keep the edge of the elastic firm against the fold of the fabric.

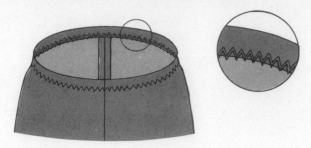

If you are using a straight stitch, sew right next to the lower edge of the elastic, stretching both thicknesses as you sew.

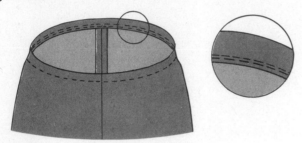

Hem

Your pants have a 1½-inch (3.8 cm) hem allowance. If you are making your first pair of pants and are unsure about the finished length, try the pants on and pin the hem in place.

Now press in the hem carefully. Even if you sew your hem by hand, a good job of pressing will add strength to the hem by keeping the hem allowance from pulling down on the stitches. Otherwise, it will look as if you jumped into your pants as soon as you finished the last seam.

You may put in your hem by hand stitching or by bonding it with *Perky Bond* fusible web. I prefer to bond my hems. It is interesting to observe a group of men or women wearing knit pants. Hems done with *Perky Bond* always look crisp and well pressed. This is not only because bonding requires careful pressing but, also, because *Perky Bond* adds body to the hem. If you are working with lightweight fabric, refer to ''Special Instructions'' at the end of the chapter for some extra tips on application.

I recommend stitching *Perky Bond* to the edge of the fabric before bonding when you are working with pant

hems or sleeve hems. Place *Perky Bond* along the lower edge of the pant leg on the wrong side. Stitch it in place ¼ inch (0.6 cm) from the cut edge.

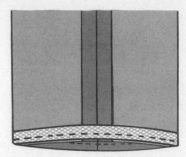

Then use a steam iron (wool setting) and a wet press cloth to bond the hem in place. Press firmly in one place for 10 or 12 seconds or until the press cloth is dry. Do not slide the iron, and make sure the iron doesn't come in touch with the *Perky Bond* because it will stick. Bond section by section, overlapping each time and rewetting the press cloth if necessary.

After the fabric has cooled, lift one edge to check the bond. If the fabric pulls away from the *Perky Bond*, repeat the procedure. If you follow these instructions, the bond should last the lifetime of your garment.

Creases after Construction

If you have waited to press creases until you were sure of the fit, you have another step to complete before you wear your new pants. Place the pants on the ironing board and fold one pant leg out of the way. On the remaining leg, match the inside leg seam to the outside leg seam, following the straight-of-grain up the center front and center back of the pant leg. There will be a little extra fullness at the upper inside leg seam as illustrated.

Use a steam iron (wool setting) and a damp press cloth. Hold the iron firmly in one place until the press cloth is dry. Repeat until you have pressed a crease in the front from the bottom of the leg up to the waist. In back, crease the pants from the bottom of the leg to crotch level. Crease the second pant leg in the same manner.

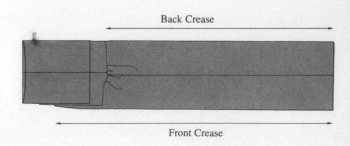
Back Crease

Front Crease

Final Pressing

The last step in constructing a beautifully-finished garment is a complete pressing. Each crease should continue into a nice sharp edge at the hem. A careful job of final pressing will usually eliminate the need for additional pressing, even after many launderings.

The Four-Gore Skirt

Preparing Your Pattern

Determining Your Pattern Size

You will trace the pattern piece for your skirt according to your hip size. Take your hip measurement 9 inches (22.9 cm) below the waist. This measurement is your hip size. Next, take a waist measurement.

Referring to the Standard Body Measurements Chart on the back of the pattern envelope, choose the size that corresponds to your hip measurement. Compare your body waist measurement to the waist measurement for your size. If your waist measurement is larger than the one given for your size, you will need to trace your pattern in a larger size at the waist.

If your waist measurement is smaller than the one given for your size, you may trace the pattern one size smaller at the waist. Remember, however, that the skirt must pull up over the hips. It's best not to trace down more than one size. Instead, rely on the elastic to draw in the waistline of your skirt.

Determine how long you want your skirt by measuring from your waistline at the center back to the desired finished skirt length. Compare this measurement to the center back length listed under the Finished Garment Measurements Chart on the back of the pattern envelope and determine whether you need to shorten or lengthen the pattern piece when you trace it.

Tracing Your Pattern Piece

Trace one Gore in your size. In order to trace a whole Gore pattern piece, fold the pattern material and place the folded edge along the "Place on Fold" line on the master pattern. You will shorten or lengthen the Gore at the pattern lower edge as you do your tracing. Maintain the original angle at the side seam and maintain the curve at the lower edge.

To Shorten   To Lengthen

Transfer all pattern markings to your tracing material.

Cutting Your Fabric

Pretreating

As usual, you will want to pretreat the fabric you have selected for your skirt. Do not pretreat the elastic.

Cutting Garment Pieces

From your fabric, cut four Gores, referring to the Suggested Cutting Layouts in the pattern instructions. If you are cutting plaid fabric or if you are cutting striped fabric which you want to chevron at the seams, refer to "Special Information" at the end of the chapter.

Remember to place the pattern pieces on the fabric so the greater stretch will go around the body in the finished garment.

You will also need to cut a strip of *Stretch & Sew* ¾-inch (1.9 cm) elastic 2 inches (5.1 cm) less than your body waist measurement.

Sewing Your Skirt

Sew your skirt right sides together with the ⅝-inch (1.6 cm) seam allowance indicated on the pattern. Unless otherwise indicated, you should use a straight stitch with 9 stitches per inch (3 mm stitch length) and stretch as you sew. As usual, I recommend that you backstitch at the beginning and end of each seam.

Skirt Seams

Place two Gores in a relaxed position on a flat surface and pin one skirt seam.

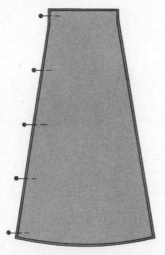

Stitch the seam, beginning at the lower edge and stretching each layer of fabric evenly as you sew.

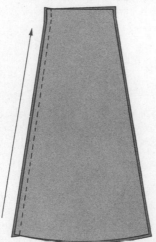

Pin and stitch each skirt seam in the same way until all the Gores have been sewn together. Then carefully press each seam open, using a damp cloth and a steam iron.

Turned-Down Elastic Waist

If you have not already cut your elastic, cut a strip of *Stretch & Sew* ¾-inch (1.9 cm) elastic 2 inches (5.1 cm) less than your body waist measurement. Lap the ends of the elastic ½ inch (1.3 cm) forming a circle, and stitch securely.

Next try on the skirt to check the fit and to establish a front and a back. The skirt may be worn with the seams at the center front, center back, and sides, or it may be worn as shown in the illustrations. Make your choice now.

Place the circle of elastic over the skirt at your waistline. Position the skirt until there is ¾ inch (1.9 cm) above the elastic all the way around.

Depending on the shape of your back, fullness may appear in the form of horizontal folds at the center back of your skirt.

If this happens, pull the skirt up in the back until the fullness disappears. Keeping the elastic at your waistline, pin the elastic in place around the skirt.

Mark the back and then remove the skirt. Trim the fabric, if necessary, around the upper edge so that there is ¾ inch (1.9 cm) above the elastic all the way around. Then remove the circle of elastic.

Divide the elastic in fourths and mark the divisions with pins. Avoid using the seam as one of your quarter divisions.

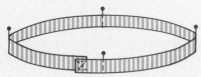

Pin the elastic to the wrong side of the skirt even with the upper edge, matching the quarter divisions to the four skirt seams.

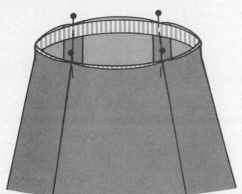

With the elastic on top and the skirt next to the sewing machine, zigzag the elastic to the skirt along the upper edge, stretching the elastic to fit the waist. Or you may use a straight stitch, but you must stretch *both* thicknesses as you sew.

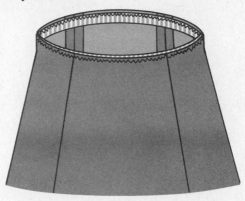

You may permanently mark the back of your skirt just as described for the pants. Cut a strip of fabric approximately ½ inch (1.3 cm) wide by 2½ inches (6.4 cm) long. Fold the strip in half and pin it in place at the center back waist edge as illustrated.

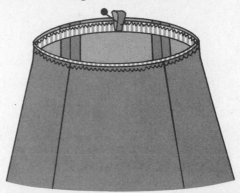

When you finish the elastic, there will be a loop on the inside of the skirt, marking the back. Or, you may wish to use a *Stretch & Sew* garment label to mark the back.

Fold the elastic to the wrong side of the skirt and pin it in place. Keep the fabric pulled straight and taut with the edge of the elastic right against the fold of the fabric.

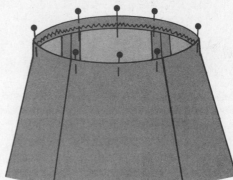

Zigzag the waistline again. This time the zigzag stitch should just overlap the lower edge of the elastic as illustrated. Stretch as you sew and keep the edge of the elastic firm against the fold of the fabric.

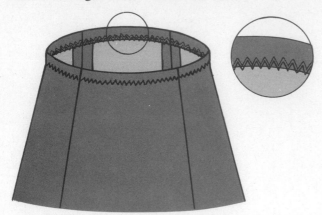

If you are using a straight stitch, sew right next to the lower edge of the elastic, stretching both thicknesses as you sew.

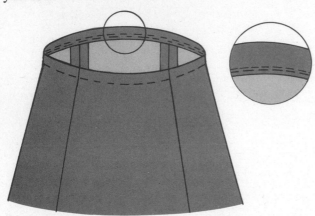

Hem

The four-gore skirt allows for a 2-inch (5.1 cm) hem. Try the skirt on and make sure it's an even length all the way around. Pin the hem in place. Then, carefully press in the hemline of the skirt.

You may put in your hem by hand stitching or by bonding it with *Perky Bond*.

To bond the hem, place strips of *Perky Bond* under the hem allowance just below the cut edge. Using a steam iron (wool setting) and a wet press cloth, press firmly in one place for 10 to 12 seconds or until the press cloth is dry. Do not slide the iron, and make sure the iron doesn't come in touch with the *Perky Bond*. Bond section by section, overlapping each time and rewetting the press cloth if necessary.

After the hem is complete, give your skirt a final pressing and it will be ready for you to wear!

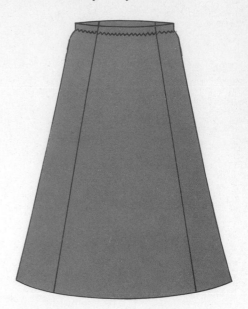

Special Information

Matching Plaids in Pants

There are many types of plaids, some of them requiring more care than others in the cutting. To match plaids, you will generally need more fabric than indicated in the yardage chart on the back of the pattern envelope. A good rule for figuring extra yardage is to allow the width of one "repeat" in the plaid pattern for every major pattern piece.

Before you cut your fabric, study the plaid to see how you want to use the pattern. If there is a dominant vertical stripe in the design, I suggest you align the straight-of-grain line along this stripe when you cut the Fronts for your pants. This will give your pants a balanced look when seen from the front.

You may wish to align the straight-of-grain line to the same dominant stripe when you cut the Backs. However, this will generally make it impossible to match vertical stripes at the side seams. If you choose to match vertical stripes at the side seams, match from seamline to seamline rather than from cut edge to cut edge. Drawing in the side seamlines on your Front and Back pattern pieces will make matching easier.

Refer to the following layout when you cut your fabric. The crotch point of each piece should be along the same horizontal stripe. Notice that the side of each Front is next to the side of its corresponding Back. This makes matching at the side seams easier. After cutting the first Front, use it as a pattern for cutting the second one. Remember to flip it over so you will have both a right and left side for your pants. Repeat for the Backs.

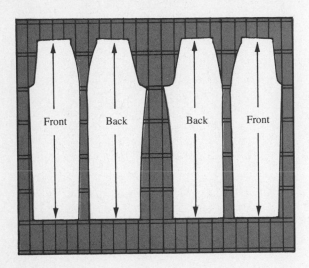

Matching Plaids in the Four-Gore Skirt

Matching plaids in the four-gore skirt is very simple. When you cut the first Gore, align the center foldline along one of the vertical stripes in the plaid. Choose the dominant vertical line in the design if there is one. Then use the first Gore as a pattern for cutting the remaining three Gores.

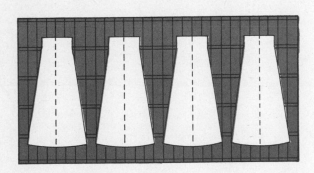

Chevroned Stripes in the Four-Gore Skirt

The four-gore skirt lends itself to striped fabric cut on the bias. If you cut your fabric correctly, the stripes will chevron at each seam. Once you learn the technique for establishing a bias line on your pattern, you will be able to use it for cutting stripes or plaids on the bias for many other garments as well.

To draw in a bias line on the Gore pattern, use a triangle ruler with a 45-degree angle as a guide. Align the ruler with the straight-of-grain as illustrated and draw in the bias line.

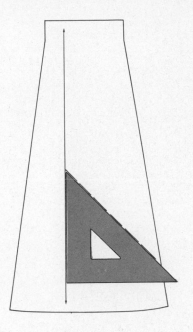

Then extend the bias line to the edges of the pattern piece to help in matching stripes.

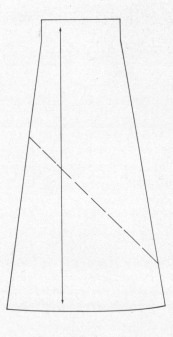

Cut one Gore from your fabric, matching the bias line along the edge of a stripe. Use this Gore as a pattern for cutting the remaining Gores, matching stripes for each one. Flip it over to cut two of the Gores.

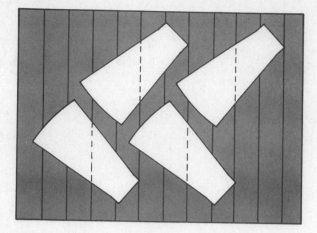

Sew the skirt according to the instructions under the heading "Sewing Your Skirt" in the earlier part of the chapter. Match stripes in a chevron pattern along each seam and position the seams at the center front, center back, and sides of the skirt. It is most slimming to have the chevrons pointing up at the center front and the center back.

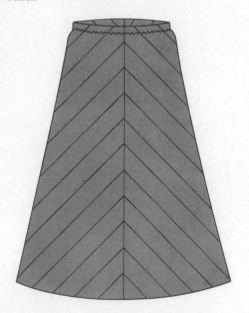

Extra Tips for Using *Perky Bond*

As you've probably guessed by now, using *Perky Bond* is my favorite way of hemming. I want to share with you some ways to ensure success when you use this product.

When you sewed your pants, you learned how to stitch *Perky Bond* in place before bonding for short hems on pant legs or sleeves. Then you are able to bond the hem quickly without spending any time positioning the *Perky Bond* under the hem allowance. When you are sewing with lightweight fabric, I recommend that you avoid this technique. It's possible that the line of stitching would be pressed into the fabric, creating a ridge visible from the right side of the garment.

If you ever have any doubts as to the finished appearance, test the *Perky Bond* on a scrap of fabric. Occasionally it's difficult to apply *Perky Bond* to a very stretchy fabric without ruffling the edge as you press.

Chapter 3
Square Neck Raglan and Raglan Turtleneck with Zipper

Introduction

The raglan has nearly become a trademark of Stretch & Sew and of *Ann Person*™ sewing techniques. There is no garment that is easier to sew than the raglan, and the square neck raglan is an absolute stroke of genius if I say so myself. Everyone who is learning to sew should have the thrill of making at least one of these great dresses.

In Class 3 you will also learn how to sew a raglan turtleneck that has a zipper without a seam. This is a method I lifted from ready-to-wear in the early days of Stretch & Sew. You will find this zipper application in many *Stretch & Sew*® patterns. Another special method you will learn in Class 3 is how to ''stitch-in-the-ditch.'' This is a technique developed by manufacturing companies.

Class 3 combines easy sewing with thrilling new techniques. I suggest you sew the square neck raglan to wear as a dress over the raglan turtleneck. Then you have all the fun and all the excitement from the raglan class combined in a stunning new ensemble for your wardrobe. Another idea to keep in mind is that the square neck raglan, shortened, is a lovely tunic to wear over pants made from *Stretch & Sew* Pattern No. 700.

M10 men
3/8 To 1 yd. short sleeves for
- 1 3/4 y

long 1 3/8 sleeve
1 5/8 dress
2 3/8 long slot sleeve
short dress

1/4 in on side of top & sleeve

Square Neck Raglan and Raglan Turtleneck with Zipper

Pattern Selection

Stretch & Sew Pattern No. 205

The square neck raglan dress you are sewing in Class 3 is View D of *Stretch & Sew* Pattern No. 205. The raglan turtleneck you will sew is a variation of View B. However, instead of the ribbing turtleneck in Pattern No. 205, you will apply a self-fabric turtleneck with a zipper. Pattern No. 205 also features square neck and crew neck raglan tops.

Pattern No. 205 has adapters for cutting a square neck-line and an adapter for extending the pattern pieces to dress length. In Class 3 you will learn how to use these handy tools to create a multipurpose pattern.

Whether you decide to make a short or long sleeve variation, a dress or a top, a square neck or a turtleneck, you will find the excitement of sewing the raglan pattern one that will give you pleasure for many garments to come.

Fabric Selection

Fabric for Your Raglan

I love the effect of striped fabric for the raglan. The use of stripes gives the garment a special look all its own. The stripes match in a chevron design at each raglan seam, forming a square to mirror the lines of the neck-line in the square neck raglan. In Class 1 you discovered stripes in cotton single knit. Now is your opportunity to find stripes in polyester blends and in a variety of other fabrics that will look lovely in the square neck raglan dress.

A raglan garment should be made from soft fabric for the best fit. I love crew neck or turtleneck sweaters made from Pattern No. 205, and jersey acrylic is the perfect fabric choice.

Percent of Stretch as It Relates to Size

Pattern No. 205 is designed to be used with fabric that has 25 percent stretch. However, cotton interlock, which has 50 percent stretch, is a very popular fabric for the raglan turtleneck. If you select cotton interlock, trace your pattern one size smaller than your regular bust size. The greater stretch of the fabric becomes ease in the garment to create a good fit from the smaller pattern size.

Yardage and Notions

After you have selected your fabric, refer to the back of the pattern envelope for yardage and notions. I recommend that you plan on using *Do-Sew*® pattern material for your tracing so that you can stitch the pattern adapters in place.

For the square neck raglan dress, you will need yardage for View D. You will also need approximately 2 yards (1.83 m) of strong string or cording in order to learn a handy technique for turning a belt right side out after you sew it.

For the raglan turtleneck with the fold-down zipper, you will need to add ⅓ yard (0.30 m) to the yardage for View B — unless you are working with 60-inch (150 cm) fabric that doesn't have a permanent crease, in which case extra yardage is not required. The extra ⅓ yard (0.30 m) is for the self-fabric turtleneck piece you will be using in place of a ribbing turtleneck. You will also need *Do-Sew* for the zipper stay, a 12-inch (30.5 cm) zipper, and ⅛-inch (0.3 cm) wide adhesive basting tape.

Square Neck Raglan

Preparing Your Pattern

Determining Your Pattern Size

Refer to the Standard Body Measurements Chart on the back of the pattern envelope and you will see that bust, waist, hip, center back length, and arm length measurements are indicated. These measurements are necessary to ensure a good fit.

Choose the size that corresponds to your bust measurement. Then compare your waist and, especially, your hip measurement to the waist and hip measurements given for your size. Do they match or will you need to trace up or down in size at the waist or hip for a good fit? Note how much, if any, you must shorten or lengthen the pattern pieces for center back waist length or for arm length.

Because the Standard Body Measurements Chart is just what it says — standard — the measurements given for your size are the same as the measurements given for your size in Pattern No. 310, for example. If your own body measurements have not changed, you will find yourself making the same adjustments now as you made when you traced your T-shirt.

I will be sharing with you a technique for preparing a pattern which may be used for both a top-length and a dress-length garment. Because of this, take center back length measurements to determine your desired finished top length and to determine your desired finished dress length.

Compare these measurements to the center back lengths given for your size in the Finished Garment Measurements Chart on the back of the pattern envelope. Note how much, if any, you will need to shorten or lengthen the pattern pieces for desired length. Take into account any amount you plan to shorten or lengthen the pattern for center back waist length, for this will affect your finished garment length.

Tracing Your Pattern Pieces

Pattern No. 205 features adapters which you will trace and attach to other pattern pieces, creating a multipurpose pattern. I recommend you use *Do-Sew* pattern material for your tracing because you will be able to stitch the adapters in place.

For your square neck raglan dress, you will need to trace in your bust size, a Front/Back, a Straight Sleeve, a Square Neck Adapter (Front/Back), a Square Neck Adapter (Sleeve), a Dress Adapter, and a Belt. To trace whole pattern pieces, fold your tracing material and place the folded edge along each "Place on Fold" line on the master pattern.

If you trace up or down in size at the waist or hip when you trace the Front/Back, make an identical adjustment on the Dress Adapter. Make adjustments, if necessary, for garment length at the pattern lower edges as you do your tracing. Transfer all pattern markings to your tracing material.

After you have cut out your pattern pieces, use the lines provided to shorten or lengthen the Front/Back for center back waist length and the Sleeve for arm length.

Attaching the Adapters

You will attach the adapters to create a pattern that may be used in many different ways. As I mentioned before, you may *stitch* the adapters in place if you are working with *Do-Sew*. With *Perky*® pattern paper, you should tape the adapters in place.

First match the Square Neck Adapter (Front/Back) to the placement line on the Front/Back pattern piece as illustrated. Secure the Adapter by stitching or taping right along the line so that it will easily fold down when you choose to cut a raglan with the round neckline.

In the same manner, attach the Square Neck Adapter (Sleeve) to the placement line on the Straight Sleeve.

Now match the Dress Adapter to the placement line on the Front/Back. Again, you should secure the Adapter right along the line so that it will fold out of the way when you cut a top-length garment.

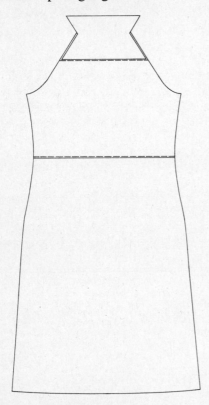

Cutting Your Fabric

Pretreating

Pretreat the fabric you have selected for your square neck raglan dress, following the care instructions which accompany the fabric.

Cutting Garment Pieces

You will need to cut two Front/Backs (using the Square Neck Adapter and the Dress Adapter), two Straight Sleeves (using the Square Neck Adapter), and one Belt. Depending on the width of your fabric, you may have to piece the Belt at the center. Follow the Suggested Cutting Layouts for View D in Pattern No. 205, and remember to place the pattern pieces on the fabric so the greater stretch will go around the body.

Matching Stripes

As I mentioned before, striped fabric enhances the square neck raglan. Make the most of your stripes by planning how you use them. For instance, choose a stripe in a flattering color to run along the square neck foldline because this color will be closest to your face. Or, if you have narrow shoulders, plan the layout so a dominant stripe will create the appearance of a broad yoke making your shoulders seem wider.

Matching stripes in the raglan is very similar to matching stripes in the T-shirt. You will match the underarms of the Front/Back to the underarms of the Sleeves. You will also match stripes along the square neck foldlines.

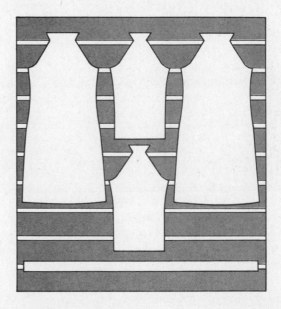

Sewing Your Square Neck Raglan

Unless otherwise indicated, you will stitch seams right sides together with a ¼-inch (0.6 cm) seam allowance. You will use a straight stitch with 9 stitches per inch (3 mm stitch length) and stretch as you sew. For reinforcement, I recommend that you backstitch at the beginning and end of each seam.

Sleeves

First pin and stitch both Sleeves to one Front/Back. Begin sewing at the underarm and stitch to the square neck foldline. Leaving the needle in the fabric, pivot the garment. Then sew to the end of the square neck facing.

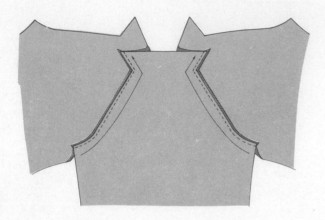

Now doublestitch these seams by sewing a second line of stitching on the seam allowance ⅛ inch (0.3 cm) from the previous line of stitching. Begin stitching at the underarm and pivot at the square neck foldline.

Sew the Sleeves to the other Front/Back in the same manner. Then press all the seam allowances toward the Sleeves.

Square Neck Facings

I have developed a technique for finishing the square neck which secures the facings and, at the same time, encloses all of the seam allowances. If you follow my instructions exactly, all of the seam allowances will end up folded toward the Sleeves.

Take one corner of the square neckline and fold both layers of the facing on the foldline *toward the Front/Back*. Pin the facing in place.

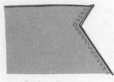   

Before Folding   After Folding

Now stitch over the previous stitching line ¼ inch (0.6 cm) from the cut edge, sewing from the foldline to the end of the facing.

Fold, pin and stitch the three remaining corners in the same manner. Remember to always fold the facing *toward the Front/Back*. Turn the square neck facing to its finished position, enclosing the seam allowances. Then press the neckline of your raglan.

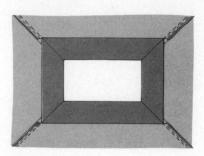

Side Seams

Pin and stitch each side seam, beginning at the lower edge of the dress and sewing up through the underarm to the lower edge of the Sleeve.

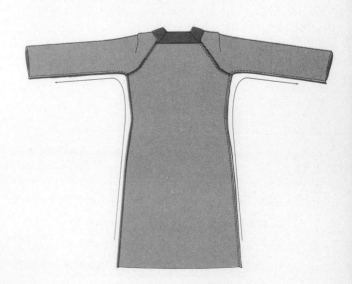

50

Now doublestitch these seams, sewing ⅛ inch (0.3 cm) from the previous line of stitching. Begin at the lower edge of the dress.

Hems

Your raglan dress has a 2-inch (5.1 cm) hem allowance. Try on the dress to check the length. Then press the hem in place and secure it by bonding with *Perky Bond®* or by hand stitching.

Press a 5-inch (12.7 cm) hem in each Sleeve and bond, hand stitch or machine stitch the hems in place.

Cuffs

Turn up a 3½-inch (8.9 cm) cuff on each Sleeve. Press the cuff, matching the seamline on the cuff to the seamline on the Sleeve. Pin the cuff in place.

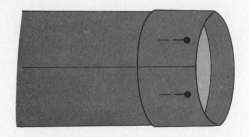

To secure the cuffs, you will learn to stitch-in-the-ditch, a nifty technique I developed for home sewers in the early days of Stretch & Sew. To stitch-in-the-ditch, you simply sew into the seam on the right side of the garment, using your regular sewing machine foot and your regular stitch length. You will be using this technique in many of the classes to come.

Place a cuff under the presser foot of your sewing machine and stitch along the seamline, sewing from the right side of the garment. Sew slowly enough to keep your stitching directly in the seamline. Secure the other cuff in the same way.

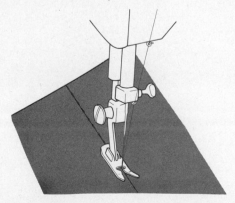

Belt

As you sew the Belt, you will learn a method I use for turning the Belt right side out after stitching the seam. For this technique, you will need a piece of strong cording or string that is at least 65 inches (165.1 cm) long.

First trim one end of the Belt piece to form a wedge approximately 1 inch (2.5 cm) deep. Place one end of the cording on the right side of the Belt along the center of the wedge as illustrated and stitch it *securely* in place.

Now turn the wedge right sides together with the Belt so that the cording lies along the center of the strip.

Fold the Belt lengthwise with right sides together and pin. Then, starting ½ inch (1.3 cm) from the wedge end, stitch the length of the Belt with a ¼-inch (0.6 cm) seam allowance. Stretch firmly as you sew and take care not to catch the wedge or the cording in your stitching.

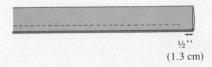

½"
(1.3 cm)

Arrange the Belt on your ironing board so that the seam is in the center of the strip. Press the seam open as illustrated.

To turn the Belt right side out, simply pull the cording from the end without the wedge. Trim away the wedge and tuck the cut edges to the inside at each end of the Belt. Secure the ends by hand stitching or by bonding with *Perky Bond*.

Give your square neck raglan a final pressing and you have completed one more garment for your class series!

Raglan Turtleneck with Fold-Down Zipper

With this raglan turtleneck, the zipper folds down with the turtleneck trim as illustrated.

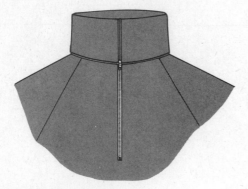

Preparing Your Pattern

Tracing Your Pattern Pieces

For your raglan turtleneck, use the same Front/Back you prepared for your square neck raglan dress. You will fold the adapters out of the way when you cut your fabric. In your bust size trace a Tapered Sleeve and a Front Neck Template from Pattern No. 205. You will use the Template to cut the front neckline on your garment *during* construction. Adjust the Sleeve, if necessary, on the line provided for shortening and lengthening.

Preparing the Zipper Stay

For your zipper without a seam, you will use a stay to guide your stitching and to stabilize the fabric while you apply the zipper. I have found that *Do-Sew*, a Stretch & Sew product normally used for tracing patterns, makes an excellent stay.

To prepare a stay to use with your 12-inch (30.5 cm) zipper, cut a rectangle of *Do-Sew* 2¼ inches (5.7 cm) wide by 8¼ inches (21.0 cm) long. Use your ruler to draw a box along the center of the rectangle as illustrated ¼ inch (0.6 cm) wide by 7¼ inches (18.4 cm) long. This box forms the stitching lines on the stay.

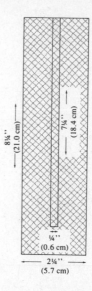

Now draw a line down the center of the box with a ¼-inch (0.6 cm) high wedge at the bottom. These lines will be cutting lines.

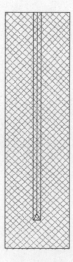

Cutting Your Fabric

Pretreating

Pretreat the fabric you have selected for your raglan turtleneck, following the care instructions which accompany the fabric.

Cutting Garment Pieces

You will need to cut two Front/Backs (folding the Square Neck Adapter and the Dress Adapter out of the way) and two Tapered Sleeves. Follow the Suggested Cutting Layouts for View B in Pattern No. 205, and remember to place the pattern pieces on the fabric so the greater stretch will go around the body. You will cut the turtleneck piece during construction.

Sewing Your Raglan Turtleneck

Unless otherwise indicated, you will stitch seams right sides together with a ¼-inch (0.6 cm) seam allowance, and you will use a straight stitch with 9 stitches per inch (3 mm stitch length), stretching as you sew. For reinforcement, I recommend that you backstitch at the beginning and end of each seam.

Stay

First mark the center of one Front/Back with pins or a *light* crease. This Front/Back will become the Back of your garment. Pin the stay to the *right* side of the back, matching center lines.

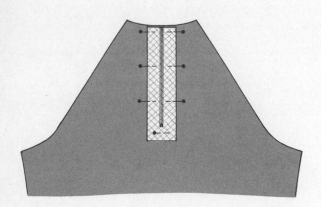

With 12 stitches per inch (2.5 mm stitch length), begin sewing at one lower corner of the box. (Do not backstitch.) Sew on the stitching line across the bottom of

the box. Then pivot and sew on the stitching line to the neck edge. Repeat for the other side, sewing across the bottom of the box a second time.

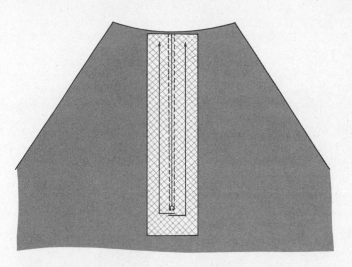

Now cut on the center line through both stay and fabric. Cut into the corners of the wedge, being careful not to cut through the stitching.

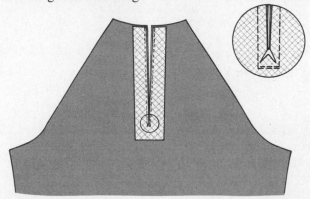

Turn the stay to the wrong side of the garment and press the stay and the seam allowances toward the center back as illustrated.

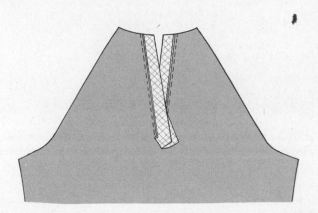

Sleeves

Beginning at the underarm, pin and stitch each Sleeve to the Front. Doublestitch these seams by sewing a second row of stitching on the seam allowance ⅛ inch (0.3 cm) from the previous line of stitching.

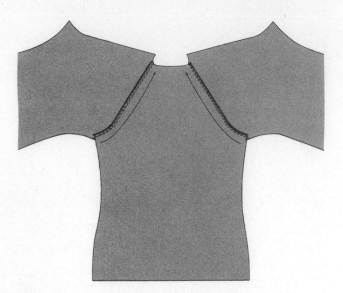

Sew the Sleeves to the Back in the same manner. Then press all the seam allowances toward the Sleeves.

Front Neckline

Fold the garment in half along the center front and center back. Pin the Front Neck Template to the Front, matching neck edges and center fronts as illustrated.

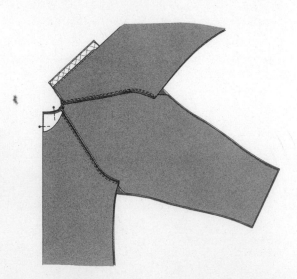

Now, using the Template as a guide, cut the neckline on the Front.

Turtleneck

To determine how long to cut your turtleneck piece, measure the neckline of the garment, beginning and ending at the stitching lines of the stay. Add ½ inch (1.3 cm) to this measurement. Cut the turtleneck piece this length by 11¼ inches (28.6 cm) deep. The greater stretch in the fabric should run the length of the strip (around the body in the finished garment).

With right sides together, pin the turtleneck piece to the neck edge of the garment with the ends of the turtleneck extending ¼ inch (0.6 cm) past the stitching lines of the stay. Stitch the turtleneck to the garment with a ¼-inch (0.6 cm) seam allowance. Press the turtleneck piece and the seam allowances toward the neck opening as illustrated.

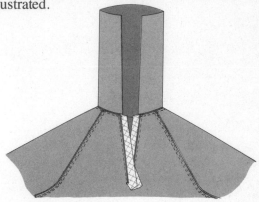

Zipper Application

Apply basting tape to the right side of the zipper tape along the outside edges.

To form a box for the zipper, turn the stay to the inside of the garment and turn back ¼ inch (0.6 cm) at each end of the turtleneck for seam allowances. The stay should not be visible from the right side of the garment.

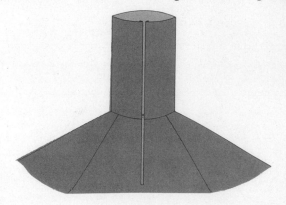

Place the zipper in its finished position behind the box. The lower edge of the metal stop should show at the bottom of the box. This metal stop guards your fabric from snags that might be caused by the zipper pull. The zipper teeth should be next to the stitching lines and they should extend 5 inches (12.7 cm) into the turtleneck piece. Finger-press the stay and the turtleneck seam allowances to the basting tape on the zipper.

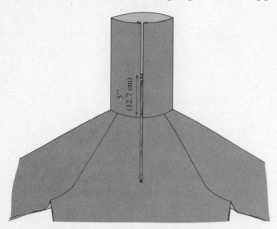

I suggest you use a zipper foot for sewing your zipper in place. Lift the Back as illustrated to expose the wedge at the bottom of the box. Stitch across the wedge through the stay and the zipper tape.

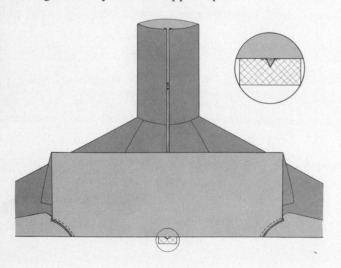

Fold the Back over as illustrated to expose the seam allowance along the side of the box. Beginning at the bottom of the box, sew next to the previous stitching, sewing on the garment side of the stitching line so your

Do-Sew won't show from the right side. Continue stitching to the top of the zipper teeth, matching the edge of the zipper tape to the cut edge of the turtleneck piece.

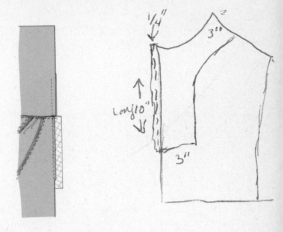

Sew the zipper to the other side of the Back in the same manner. Then remove the basting tape and trim the stay even with the edges of the zipper tape.

Unzip the zipper and turn the zipper tape toward the center back. At the top of the zipper, fold the ends of the zipper tape toward the seam allowances as illustrated. Do not cut them off because they will fray.

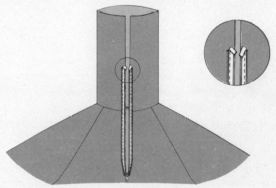

On each side of the zipper, fold the turtleneck piece right sides together over the zipper tape and pin it in place. A ¾-inch (1.9 cm) seam allowance should extend past the neckline seam of the garment.

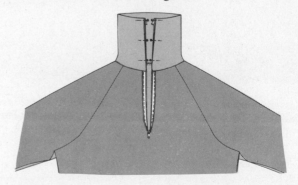

To stitch, turn the turtleneck to expose the original stitching line. Stitch again on this line, sewing through the two layers of turtleneck fabric and through the zipper tape which is sandwiched between them. Sew to ⅛ inch (0.3 cm) below the neckline seam as illustrated. Repeat for the other side of the zipper.

Be sure to catch the seam allowance of the turtleneck in this stitching. Sew slowly enough to keep your stitching directly in the seam.

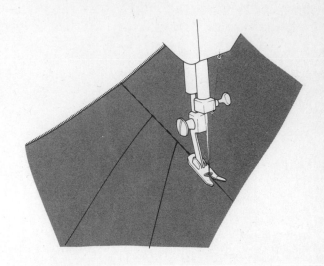

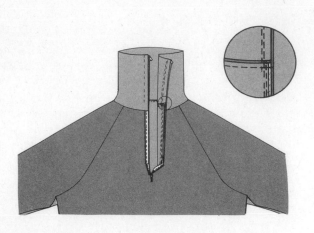

On the wrong side of the garment, trim the turtleneck seam allowance to ⅛ inch (0.3 cm) from the stitching.

Side Seams

Pin and stitch each side seam, beginning at the lower edge of the garment and sewing through the underarm to the lower edge of the Sleeve. Doublestitch these seams by sewing a second row of stitching on the seam allowance ⅛ inch (0.3 cm) from the previous stitching.

Turtleneck Finish

Fold the turtleneck right side out, exposing the zipper teeth. Arrange the turtleneck piece so the cut edge extends ¾ inch (1.9 cm) past the seam all the way around the neckline. Pin the turtleneck in place, pinning from the right side.

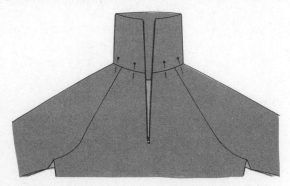

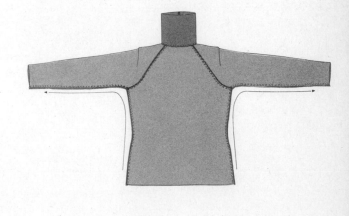

To secure the turtleneck you will stitch-in-the-ditch. Place the neckline of your raglan turtleneck under the presser foot of your sewing machine and stitch along the seamline, sewing from the right side of the garment.

Hems

Press a 1-inch (2.5 cm) hem in each Sleeve and a 1½-inch (3.8 cm) hem at the lower edge of the garment. Secure the hems by bonding with *Perky Bond,* machine stitching, or hand stitching.

Give your raglan turtleneck a final pressing and it's complete!

Special Information

Raglan with Zipper to Fold of Turtleneck

The raglan turtleneck described previously has a zipper that folds down with the turtleneck. Another popular look is for the zipper to extend only to the fold of the finished turtleneck as illustrated.

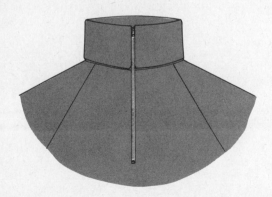

For a turtleneck with a zipper to the fold, follow the instructions given previously for the turtleneck with a fold-down zipper *except* you will need a 9-inch (22.9 cm) zipper. And, the instructions under the headings "Preparing the Zipper Stay" and "Zipper Application" do not apply. For these steps, follow the instructions below.

Preparing the Zipper Stay

Cut a stay from *Do-Sew* 2¼ inches (5.7 cm) wide by 7¾ inches (19.7 cm) long. Draw a box along the center of the stay ¼ inch (0.6 cm) wide by 6¾ inches (17.1 cm) long as illustrated. Then draw a line down the center of the box with a ¼-inch (0.6 cm) high wedge at the bottom.

Zipper Application

After you have sewn the turtleneck piece to the neck edge of the garment, you will fold it as described here before you begin applying the zipper. First fold the turtleneck piece wrong sides together so there are 5 inches (12.7 cm) between the neckline seam and the fold. On the inside, a ¾-inch (1.9 cm) seam allowance should extend past the neckline seam.

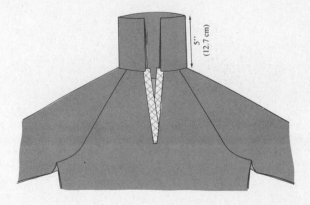

Next fold the turtleneck in its finished position, matching the fold to the neckline seam.

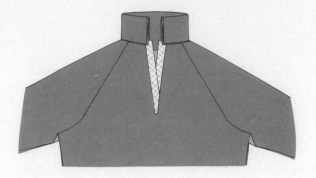

Then fold up the inside layer of the turtleneck piece as illustrated. Pin the turtleneck to hold it in place while you apply the zipper.

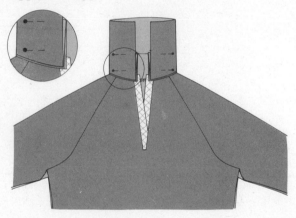

Apply basting tape to the right side of the zipper tape along the outside edges.

To form a box for the zipper, turn the stay to the inside of the garment and turn back ¼ inch (0.6 cm) at each end of the turtleneck for seam allowances. The stay should not be visible from the right side of the garment.

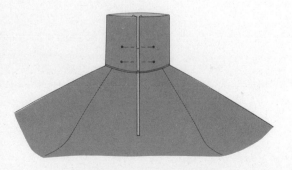

Place the zipper in its finished position behind the box. The lower edge of the metal stop should show at the bottom of the box and the zipper teeth should be next to the stitching lines. The zipper teeth should extend 2½ inches (6.4 cm) into the turtleneck piece. Finger-press the stay and the turtleneck seam allowances to the basting tape on the zipper.

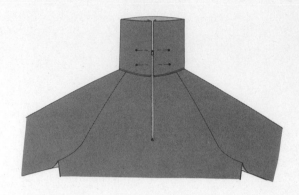

I suggest you use a zipper foot for sewing your zipper in place. Lift the Back as illustrated to expose the wedge at the bottom of the box. Stitch across the wedge through the stay and the zipper tape.

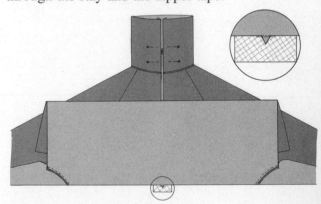

Fold the Back over as illustrated to expose the seam allowance along the side of the box. Beginning at the bottom of the box, sew next to the previous stitching, sewing on the garment side of the stitching line so your *Do-Sew* won't show from the right side. Continue stitching to the top of the zipper teeth, matching the edge of the zipper tape to the cut edges of the turtleneck piece.

Sew the other side of the zipper in the same manner. Then remove the basting tape and trim the stay even with the edges of the zipper tape.

Unzip the zipper and turn the zipper tape toward the center back. At the top of the zipper, fold the ends of the zipper tape toward the seam allowances as illustrated. Do not cut them off or they will fray.

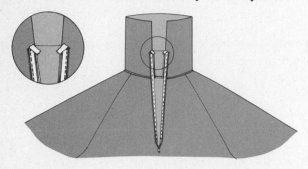

On each side of the zipper, fold the turtleneck piece right sides together over the zipper tape and pin it in place. A ¾-inch (1.9 cm) seam allowance should extend past the neckline seam of the garment.

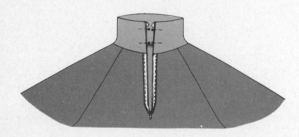

To stitch, turn the turtleneck to expose the original stitching line. Stitch again on this line, sewing through the four layers of turtleneck fabric and through the zipper tape which is sandwiched between them. Sew to ⅛ inch (0.3 cm) below the neckline seam as illustrated. Repeat for the other side of the zipper.

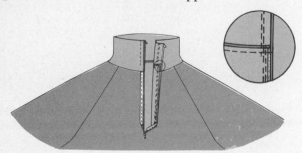

Finish the turtleneck and complete the garment just as you would sew the raglan turtleneck with the fold-down zipper described earlier in the chapter.

Modifying the Turtleneck and Zipper Application

Turtleneck Depth

The turtleneck described in this chapter is 2½ inches (6.4 cm) deep when finished. Here's a formula for figuring how wide to cut the turtleneck piece for a turtleneck of a different depth:

Multiply the desired finished depth times four, and add 1¼ inches (3.2 cm). The 1¼ inches (3.2 cm) provides the necessary seam allowances plus ¼ inch (0.6 cm) for folding ease.

When you adjust the depth of the turtleneck, you must also refigure the length of the zipper stay as described below.

Adjusting Stay for Zipper Length or Turtleneck Depth

You may, of course, use a longer length zipper for your turtleneck than the lengths recommended in this chapter — which are 12 inches (30.5 cm) for the fold-down zipper technique and 9 inches (22.9 cm) for the zipper-to-fold technique.

But when you change the length of the zipper, you must change the length of the zipper stay and of the box on the stay. You must also change these dimensions when you adjust the depth of the turtleneck. Here are formulas for figuring the correct length for the stay and of the box:

For the fold-down zipper technique, determine the length of the zipper by measuring the zipper teeth from the bottom of the metal stop to the top of the zipper pull. Subtract *twice* the desired finished turtleneck depth from the length of the zipper. Then add ¼ inch (0.6 cm) for seam allowance. This gives you the length for the box. Add 1 inch (2.5 cm) to the length of the box to get the length for the stay itself. Cut the stay 2½ inches (6.4 cm) wide, as usual, and draw the box ¼ inch (0.6 cm) wide.

For example, let us suppose that your zipper measures 14 inches (35.6 cm) and you want a 3-inch (7.6 cm) finished turtleneck depth. Double the turtleneck depth and you have 6 inches (15.2 cm). Subtract 6 inches (15.2 cm) from 14 inches (35.6 cm) and you have 8 inches (20.3 cm). Then, add ¼ inch (0.6 cm) for a box length of 8¼ inches (21.0 cm). Add 1 inch (2.5 cm) for the length of the stay.

For the zipper-to-fold technique, determine the length of the zipper by measuring the zipper teeth from the bottom of the metal stop to the top of the zipper pull. Subtract the desired finished turtleneck depth from this measurement. Then add ¼ inch (0.6 cm) for seam allowance. This gives you the length for the box. Add 1 inch (2.5 cm) to the length of the box to get the length for the stay itself. Cut the stay 2½ inches (6.4 cm) wide, as usual, and draw the box ¼ inch (0.6 cm) wide.

For example, let us suppose that your zipper measures 14 inches (35.6 cm) and you want a 3-inch (7.6 cm) finished turtleneck depth. Subtract 3 inches (7.6 cm) from 14 inches (35.6 cm) and you have 11 inches (27.9 cm). Then add ¼ inch (0.6 cm) for a box length of 11¼ inches (28.6 cm). Add 1 inch (2.5 cm) for the length of the stay.

Wide-Toothed Decorative Zipper at Center Front

A very popular look is the zipper into a turtleneck (using the fold-down zipper technique) with the zipper sewn into the center front of the garment. This is especially attractive with a wide-toothed decorative zipper. (You may also want to use a deeper turtleneck or a longer zipper as described above.)

There are two things to keep in mind when applying a wide-toothed zipper in the front of the raglan. First you will have to widen the box on the stay to equal the width of the zipper teeth plus ⅛ inch (0.3 cm). Next you will wait to sew the stay to the Front until you have sewn the raglan sleeve seams and cut the front neckline. Then simply follow the instructions given in the earlier part of the chapter for the turtleneck with the fold-down zipper.

Chapter 4
The Basic Dress and Blouse

Introduction

We have selected the basic dress and blouse for Class 4 because we felt that at this time in your classes you would enjoy sewing a garment that has a dart. A dart creates a more fitted shape in a garment. The need for a dart in knits is not as great as in wovens because of the built-in ease of knit fabrics, so you may notice that the dart is not as large as some you have sewn in the past.

One of the wonderful techniques that I discovered in the very early years of Stretch & Sew was how to adjust a dart very easily. In Class 4 you will learn how to position the bust dart to fit your figure perfectly. This simple technique has been a blessing to our students.

You will also learn how to apply Chanel trim to finish the neckline of the dress and the blouse. This is a technique I learned by examining ready-to-wear, but it will work only with knit fabrics. Knits have the stretch necessary to conform to the curve at the neckline and, since they don't ravel, knits require no additional finishing on the underside of the trim.

In Class 4 you will be introduced to *Stretch & Sew*® print fabrics and the very special advantages they have to offer. When I think back to the very first *Stretch & Sew*® store and remember how difficult it was to find fabrics that worked well together, I realize all of the benefits that Stretch & Sew has today because of the wonderful growth we have enjoyed. I must take this opportunity to say, ''Thank you. Thank you for being our customer and thank you for the part you have played in the growth of Stretch & Sew.''

The Basic Dress and Blouse

Pattern Selection

Stretch & Sew® Pattern No. 1505

In Class 4 you will learn how to sew two views of *Stretch & Sew* Pattern No. 1505. View A, the basic dress, has long sleeves and a scooped neckline. View C is a sleeveless blouse with a jewel neckline and a zipper without a seam in back. Since you learned the technique for a zipper without a seam in Class 3, sewing the zipper in your blouse will be a snap.

With Pattern No. 1505 you will be preparing a multipurpose pattern just as you did for your raglan in Class 3. There is a Dress Adapter for cutting a Front and Back at dress length. And, there are adapters for raising the neckline and for cutting the higher, closer armhole required for the sleeveless finish in View C.

Fabric Selection

Fabric for the Basic Dress and Blouse

The basic dress is a classic garment which will give you a variety of looks, depending on your fabric choice. It can be sewn up in solids, stripes, plaids, or prints and it is a garment for all seasons. Select a mediumweight fabric such as poly/wool double knit for fall/winter or a lightweight fabric for spring/summer.

Because the dress is so perfect for showing off prints, I want to take this opportunity to share the way *Stretch & Sew* prints are created. There are some very special advantages to *Stretch & Sew* prints. For instance, the fabrics that we choose for the base cloth in our prints are very closely monitored to ensure the excellence in quality that has become a recognized standard of Stretch and Sew.

The exciting part of the print story is that the colors are especially selected and created to give you totally coordinated ensembles. Many print designs are recolored so they will carry at least two or three of the basic

Stretch & Sew colors for the season. This is a very exciting addition to all of the wonderful advantages *Stretch & Sew Fabric*™ centers offer, and is something that has just been possible in the last few years.

There are a number of different methods for printing. One is called roller printing. This method is often used on cotton single knits. Usually great quantities of fabric are printed at one time when the roller method is used. Giant rollers with dyes applied to them transfer the design to the cloth.

Screen printing is used with knit fabrics a great deal. Dyes are blown or pushed through the screens, one color at a time. There are machine screens and hand screens. Of course, the hand screen is a more expensive method but it allows more control and a greater variety of colors.

Finally, a new method of printing that has been developed in recent years is heat transfer printing. With this method the print is applied to paper first. Then the fabric and the paper are fed through a machine while heat transfers the print from the paper to the cloth. This method is also referred to as dry printing.

Heat transfer printing is only possible on synthetic fabrics at this time and is most often used with fabrics that have a high percentage of polyester. One of the great advantages of heat transfer printing is the ability to create prints that are detailed and fine in their design. The transfer to the cloth is perfect. Because the print is transferred by heat and the fibers are synthetic, a slight melting occurs on the surface of the fabric during the process. If the fabric has been knit from a very fine yarn in a close stitch, this melting will create a silky smoothness to the surface of the fabric.

Some interesting effects are created when fabric with a mixture of fibers is printed by the heat transfer method. An example would be a polyester knit with a silk slub. The polyester yarns will take the print and the silk will not, so the design is muted for a softer look in the print.

Each season the trends in prints change with the fashion, and *Stretch & Sew* prints are influenced as are those of the rest of the fashion world. But we have added one dimension — I feel that I know our customer, and I always try to keep you in mind when I am selecting a color or design. I want to be sure that our fashion fabrics are in harmony with your tastes.

When I studied painting at the University of Oregon as a girl of fourteen, little did I know that my early interest in color and design would lead me in the direction that this wonderful company has taken me. I hope you enjoy each season as I do, with the additions of new color variations and design concepts. Fashion is exciting and it is fun to be part of this ever-changing field.

Yardage and Notions

After you have selected fabric for your dress, refer to the back of the pattern envelope for yardage and notions.

The Basic Dress
Preparing Your Pattern

Determining Your Pattern Size

Refer to the back of the Pattern No. 1505 envelope and choose the size that corresponds to your bust measurement. Check the measurement charts to determine any necessary pattern adjustments. Check center back length for both top-length and dress-length garments because you will be preparing a dual-purpose pattern.

If you are making any adjustments, I suggest you jot them down to keep in mind as you trace your pattern. Notice how automatic this process of determining how to prepare a pattern to fit your figure has become.

Tracing Your Pattern Pieces

For your basic dress, trace a Front, a Back, a Sleeve, two Dress Adapters, and a Belt. Mark the dot given in your size for the point of the bust dart, but do not draw in the dart lines at this time.

The back waistline darts are not featured in View A, but I recommend that you trace them on your Back pattern piece now for future use in the other views. These darts have been drawn for size 30 only. If you are a different size, mark the dots for your size. Then shift the tracing material, aligning the traced dots to the size 30 dots on the master pattern. Trace the dart.

Make any necessary pattern adjustments and transfer all pattern markings to your tracing material.

Bust Dart Adjustment

I have perfected a method for determining how well the dart will fit and making any necessary adjustments *before* you sew your dress. Check this now by taking two body measurements. First measure across your bust from high point to high point. Next measure from the center of your shoulder to your high point. To make sure you are measuring from the exact center, wear a Stretch & Sew T-shirt and measure from the shoulder seam at the point where your bra strap crosses your shoulder.

High Point to High Point   Shoulder to High Point

Note the difference, if any, between your measurements and those given for your size on the chart below. Bust sizes 46 through 56 have been provided for those who are sewing a Queen size pattern with a dart.

Standard High Point Measurements Chart

Bust Size	High Point to High Point	Shoulder to High Point
30	7 in. (17.8 cm)	9 in. (22.9 cm)
32	7¼ in. (18.4 cm)	9¼ in. (23.5 cm)
34	7½ in. (19.1 cm)	9½ in. (24.1 cm)
36	7¾ in. (19.7 cm)	9¾ in. (24.8 cm)
38	8 in. (20.3 cm)	10 in. (25.4 cm)
40	8¼ in. (21.0 cm)	10¼ in. (26.0 cm)
42	8½ in. (21.6 cm)	10½ in. (26.7 cm)
44	8¾ in. (22.2 cm)	10¾ in. (27.3 cm)
46	9 in. (22.9 cm)	11⅛ in. (28.3 cm)
48	9¼ in. (23.5 cm)	11½ in. (29.2 cm)
50	9½ in. (24.1 cm)	11⅞ in. (30.2 cm)
52	9¾ in. (24.8 cm)	12¼ in. (31.1 cm)
54	10 in. (25.4 cm)	12⅝ in. (32.1 cm)
56	10¼ in. (26.0 cm)	13 in. (33.0 cm)

If your body high-point-to-high-point measurement matches the measurement on the chart, the dart indicated on the pattern for your size will be the correct length. In other words, when you wear your dress, the dart will end 1½ inches (3.8 cm) from your bust high point. Draw in each dart by connecting the dot for your size to the notches on the side of the pattern.

If the measurements do not match, you will need to create a dart that is the correct length. While you make your dart adjustments, I suggest you work with half the pattern. After you have completed an adjustment, it will be a simple matter to transfer it to the other side.

First draw a horizontal line through the dot on the pattern. This line must be perpendicular to the straight-of-grain line as illustrated.

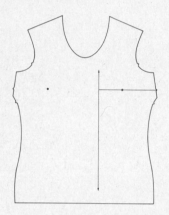

If your body high-point-to-high-point measurement is greater than the one on the chart, you will need a shorter dart. Divide in half the difference between measurements. Subtract this amount from the length of the dart by marking a new dot on the horizontal line. For example, if your body measurement is 1 inch (2.5 cm) greater than the measurement on the chart, mark a new dot on the horizontal line ½ inch (1.3 cm) toward the side of the pattern. To draw in the dart, connect this new dot to the notch on the side of the pattern.

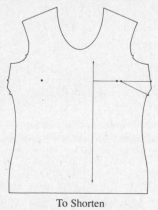

To Shorten

If your body high-point-to-high-point measurement is smaller than the one on the chart, you will need a longer dart. Divide in half the difference between measurements. Add this amount to the length of the dart by marking a new dot on the horizontal line. For example, if your body measurement is 1 inch (2.5 cm) smaller than the measurement on the chart, mark a new dot on the horizontal line ½ inch (1.3 cm) toward the center front of the pattern. To draw in the dart, connect this new dot to the notch on the side of the pattern.

To Lengthen

After you have adjusted the length of your dart, fold the pattern piece in half along the center front line and trace the dart on the other side.

If your body shoulder-to-high-point measurement matches the measurement for your size on the chart, the darts you have drawn on the pattern for your size will be the correct level for your bust line. They will not be too high or too low.

If these measurements do not match, an adjustment will be necessary. First draw a box around the dart on half your pattern as illustrated.

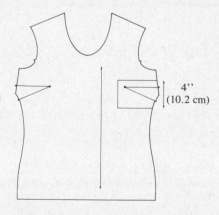

4"
(10.2 cm)

If your body shoulder-to-high-point measurement is greater than the one on the chart, you will need a lower dart. Cut along all three lines of the box and lower the dart the difference between measurements. For example, if your body measurement is 1 inch (2.5 cm) greater, lower the dart box 1 inch (2.5 cm). Tape the box in its new position.

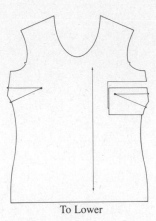

To Lower

If your body shoulder-to-high-point measurement is smaller than the one on the chart, you will need a higher dart. For example, if your body measurement is 1 inch (2.5 cm) smaller, raise the dart box 1 inch (2.5 cm). Tape the box in its new position.

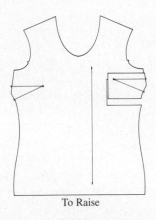

To Raise

After you have adjusted the level of your dart, back the opening in the pattern with tracing material. Then adjust the dart on the other side to the same level. Fold the pattern piece in half along the center front line to double check for accuracy. It's important that both darts are at the same level.

Attaching the Adapters

Match one of the Dress Adapters to the placement line on the Front as illustrated. Secure the Dress Adapter by stitching or taping right along the line so that it will easily fold out of the way when you choose to cut a top-length Front.

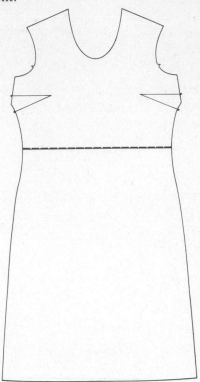

In the same manner, attach the other Dress Adapter to the Back.

Cutting Your Fabric

Pretreating

As usual, you will want to pretreat the fabric you have selected for your dress, following the care instructions which accompany the fabric.

Cutting Garment Pieces

If you are working with printed or striped fabric, I suggest that you read the special tips under the headings that follow before you actually cut into your fabric. You will find the additional information very helpful.

From your fabric, cut one Front and one Back (using the Dress Adapters), two Sleeves, and one Belt. Depending on the width of your fabric, you may have to piece the Belt at the center. Follow the Suggested Cutting

Layouts for View A in Pattern No. 1505, and remember to place the pattern pieces on the fabric so the greater stretch will go around the body in the finished garment. If you're cutting one Sleeve at a time, turn the pattern over to cut the second one, so you will have a right and left Sleeve for your dress.

You will also need to cut a Chanel strip 2½ inches (6.4 cm) wide by 30 inches (76.2 cm) long for the neckline trim. It is important that you cut the Chanel strip with the greater stretch running the length of the strip.

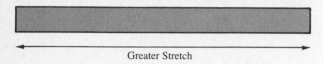
Greater Stretch

Transfer all construction marks to your fabric. I suggest you use the *Stretch & Sew*™ fabric marker for this purpose, especially for marking the darts.

Cutting Printed Fabric

Study your printed fabric carefully before you cut out your garment pieces. Does it have a one-way or two-way design? When the fabric has a two-way design, it looks the same from whichever end you view it.

If your fabric has a one-way design, you *must* lay all the pattern pieces in the same direction. This is because the design appears different viewed from one end than it does from the other.

Some one-way prints are based on natural objects. These prints must be cut so the design is right side up in the garment. You wouldn't want upside-down flowers or trees in your dress. Be aware of one-way prints based on natural objects which are highly stylized. You might not recognize the design until it's too late.

You should also take a look at the design in prints to see if you can cut the fabric in some special way to flatter your figure. When the boldness of a print varies throughout the piece, use the more dominant parts of the design to focus attention where you want it. For example, if you are large busted, you wouldn't center large flowers at the bustline. Instead, you would shift them up or down. In other words, accentuate the positive and eliminate or at least minimize the negative.

Although the border in a border print is often placed at the hem and sleeve edges of a garment, you might want the border to run across the shoulders instead. This is very effective if you have narrow shoulders in proportion to the rest of your body. Another effective use of border prints is to run the design vertically in the garment to lead the eye up and down for a slimming look.

The same principle applies to a geometric print which grows progressively larger from one end of the fabric to the other. If you have narrow shoulders and wide hips, use the larger part of the design for the upper part of the garment. If you are broad in the shoulders and small through the hips, you can afford to use the larger part of the design for the lower part of the garment.

Cutting Striped Fabric

Matching stripes in the basic dress is very similar to matching stripes in the T-shirt. However, because of the bust dart, there are some differences.

You can match the Front to the Back along the side seams from the lower edge of the garment to the lower dart notch. You cannot match stripes above the dart, but that part of the side seam is so inconspicuous that it doesn't matter.

Since the Front and Back do not match at the underarm, you cannot match the Sleeve to both the Front and the Back. Match the stripe at the underarm point on the Front to the front underarm point of each Sleeve. Then the stripes at the armhole will match when seen from the front. Center the Belt on the stripe of your choice.

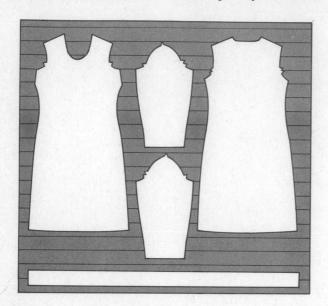

Sewing Your Basic Dress

Unless otherwise indicated, stitch seams right sides together with a ⅝-inch (1.6 cm) seam allowance. You will use a straight stitch with 9 stitches per inch (3 mm stitch length) and stretch as you sew. For reinforcement, I recommend that you backstitch at the beginning and end of each seam.

Darts

We'll begin with the darts. Fold each bust dart along the center and pin. Sew the darts, starting at the notches and stitching in a straight line to the point. Then tie off each dart at the point. Be careful not to pull the threads or you'll pucker the dart. Press the darts down.

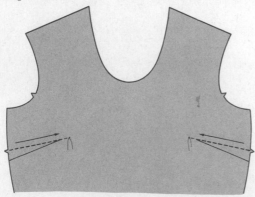

If you have marked your darts with a *Stretch & Sew* fabric marker, rinse away the ink at this time. Use a cloth thoroughly moistened with plain water.

Shoulder Seams

Pin and stitch each shoulder seam, starting at the armhole and stitching toward the neck edge.

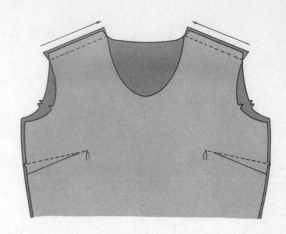

Press the shoulder seams open and trim the seam allowances even with the neck edge.

Chanel Neckline Trim

The neckline of your dress is finished with Chanel trim. When you sew the Chanel strip to the neckline of the garment, you will stretch the strip slightly. When I am doing this, I think of myself as eliminating the slack in the strip.

You stretch the trim this slight amount whenever you apply it to a curved edge. The stretching allows the finished trim to contour to the inside edge of the curve. The secret to beautifully applied Chanel trim is stretching the trim just right as you sew it to the garment. If you stretch too much, the trim will draw in the curved edge and may even pucker the garment. If you don't stretch enough to remove the slack in the trim fabric, the trim will stand away from the garment instead of following the curve as it should.

To ensure good-looking trim on your first dress, I suggest you cut a Front and Back neckline and a Chanel strip from your fabric scraps. Sew the shoulder seams and practice the trim application. There is no better way to learn than by doing. After you are feeling confident with how much to stretch, apply the trim to your basic dress.

First, fold the garment in half to find the center back. Measure 3 inches (7.6 cm) from each side of the center back and mark the neckline with pins.

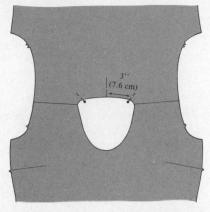

Mark the Chanel strip 3¾ inches (9.5 cm) from one end. With right sides together, match this point on the Chanel strip to one of the pins on the neck edge as illustrated.

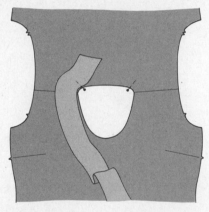

With the Chanel strip on top and the garment next to the sewing machine, stitch the Chanel strip to the neckline. Stitch from one pin, around the Front neckline, to the other pin, using a ⅜-inch (1.0 cm) seam allowance. You should not stretch the neck edge of the garment, but stretch the strip slightly to eliminate the slack in the fabric.

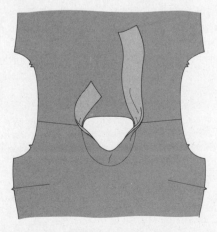

Now trim the remaining end of the Chanel strip, leaving 3¾ inches (9.5 cm) extending. To splice the Chanel strip, place the ends of the strip right sides together at a 90-degree angle and stitch as illustrated.

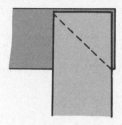

Trim the seam allowances to ¼ inch (0.6 cm) from your stitching. Press the seam open.

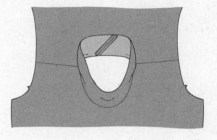

Complete the stitching, stretching the Chanel strip to fit the back neckline. Then carefully press the Chanel strip and the seam allowances toward the neck opening.

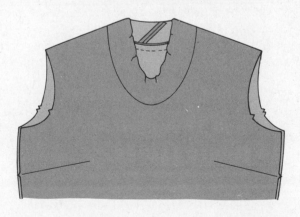

Fold the Chanel strip over the seam allowances to the wrong side of the garment. The fold of the trim should be right against the cut edges of the seam allowances. Pin the trim in place.

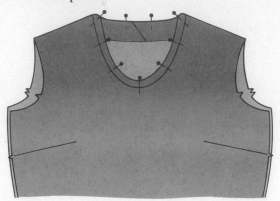

Secure the trim by stitching-in-the-ditch as you learned in Class 3. Sew into the seamline on the right side of the garment, catching the trim on the underside in your stitching.

On the wrong side of the garment, trim the extra Chanel strip to ⅛ inch (0.3 cm) from the stitching. Press the trim and the neckline is complete!

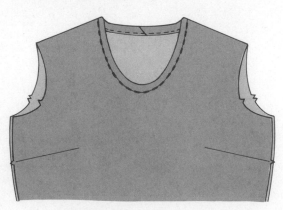

You have learned a technique which you will use again and again. I consider finishing garment edges with Chanel trim one of the most exciting things I have ever learned in my sewing.

Side Seams

You're back on familiar ground. Beginning at the lower edge of the dress, pin and stitch each side seam. Remember to stretch as you sew.

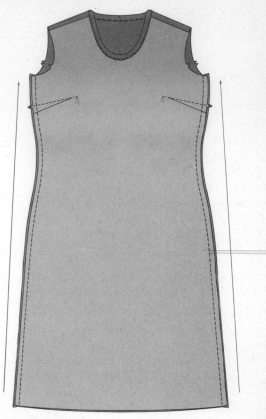

Press the seams open.

Sleeves

You will be "setting in" the Sleeves on your basic dress. If your fabric has little vertical stretch, machine baste two rows of gathering stitches ½ inch (1.3 cm) and ¾ inch (1.9 cm) from the edge of the Sleeve cap between the notches. This will help you ease the fullness of the Sleeve cap into the armhole.

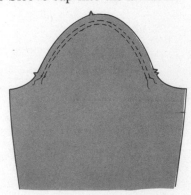

Pin and stitch the Sleeve seam, beginning at the lower edge. Press the seam open.

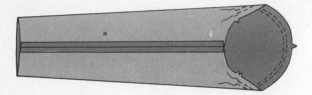

Pin the Sleeve to its armhole, matching Front and Back notches and matching the notch on the Sleeve cap to the shoulder seam. If you gathered the Sleeve cap, pull slightly on the bobbin threads of the basting stitches to ease the fullness of the Sleeve cap to fit the armhole. Then with the Sleeve on top and the garment next to the sewing machine, stitch the Sleeve to the armhole. If you did not gather the Sleeve cap, stitch with the garment on top and the Sleeve next to the sewing machine. Stretch the garment fabric slightly and allow the teeth in the machine to ease the Sleeve cap into the armhole.

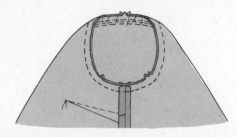

Doublestitch by sewing a second row of stitching on the seam allowance ⅛ inch (0.3 cm) from the previous stitching. Remove the basting stitches from the Sleeve cap and trim the seam allowances ⅛ inch (0.3 cm) from the second row of stitching.

Next, with the Sleeve on top and the garment next to the ironing board, steam the seam allowances as illustrated. This will ease the fullness of the Sleeve, creating a smooth seam.

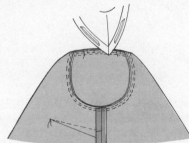

Then set in the second Sleeve in the same manner as the first.

Hems

Your basic dress has a 1-inch (2.5 cm) hem allowance in the Sleeves and a 2-inch (5.1 cm) hem at the lower edge of the garment. Try on the dress to check the length. Then press the hem in place and secure it by bonding with *Perky Bond*® fusible web or by hand stitching.

Belt

You may wish to sew the Belt with cording inside to help with turning as you learned in your last class. In that case, refer to Chapter Three for the technique.

Here are general instructions for constructing the Belt for the basic dress. Fold the Belt in half lengthwise. Then pin and stitch the length of the Belt with a ⅜-inch (1.0 cm) seam allowance. With the seam in the center of the Belt as illustrated, press the seam open.

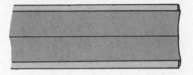

Turn the Belt right side out. Press the Belt again with the seam in the center. Fold the cut edges to the inside of the Belt. Bond with *Perky Bond* or hand stitch to finish the ends of the Belt.

Press your dress and it's ready to wear! It was simple to sew and, now that your pattern is traced and you're familiar with the techniques, you could sew a second dress in no time at all!

The Basic Blouse

Preparing Your Pattern

Tracing Your Pattern Pieces

For your basic blouse use the Front and Back you prepared for the basic dress. You will fold the Dress Adapters out of the way when you cut your fabric. For the jewel neckline and the higher, more fitted armhole for the sleeveless finish in your blouse, trace a Front View C Adapter and a Back View C Adapter. You will also need to trace the Stay on *Do-Sew* to use in applying the zipper without a seam.

Attaching the Adapters

Match the Front View C Adapter to the placement line on the Front as illustrated. Secure the Adapter by stitching or taping right along the line so it will easily fold out of the way when you choose to cut the Front without the View C Adapter.

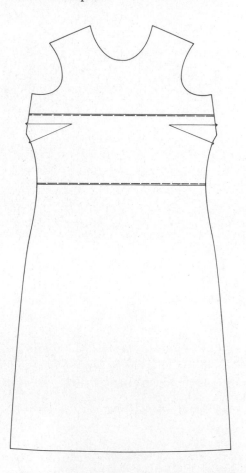

Attach the Back View C Adapter to the Back in the same way.

Cutting Your Fabric

Pretreating

Pretreat the fabric you have selected for your basic blouse, following the care instructions which accompany the fabric.

Cutting Garment Pieces

You will need to cut a Front and a Back, using the View C Adapters and folding the Dress Adapters out of the way. Follow the Suggested Cutting Layouts for View C in Pattern No. 1505, and remember to place the pattern pieces on the fabric so the greater stretch will go around the body in the finished garment. Transfer all construction marks to your fabric.

You will also need to cut a Chanel strip 2½ inches (6.4 cm) wide by 26 inches (66.0 cm) long for the neckline trim. The greater stretch in the fabric should run the length of the strip.

Sewing Your Basic Blouse

Unless otherwise indicated, stitch seams right sides together with a ⅝-inch (1.6 cm) seam allowance. You will use a straight stitch with 9 stitches per inch (3 mm stitch length) and stretch as you sew. For reinforcement, I recommend that you backstitch at the beginning and end of each seam.

Neckline

Before you begin sewing, trim ⅝ inch (1.6 cm) from the neck edges on the Front and Back garment pieces. This seam allowance is not required for the Chanel trim finish. It has been added to Pattern No. 1505 for those who want to apply the tab and collar from *Stretch & Sew* Pattern No. 1560. You will be working with this pattern in Class 6.

Darts

Fold each bust dart along the center and pin. Sew the darts, starting at the notches and stitching in a straight line to the point. Then tie off each dart at the point. Press the darts down.

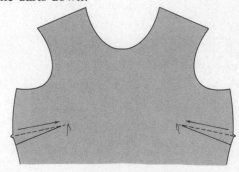

Fold each back waistline dart along the center and pin. Beginning at the waist, stitch to the upper point of the dart. Then, overlapping stitches at the waist, stitch to the lower point. Tie off the darts at the points and press them toward the center back.

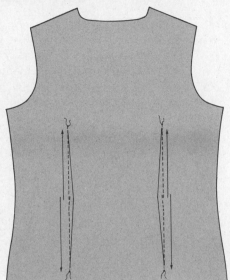

Stay

You will sew a stay to the Back just as you did for the zipper without a seam in Class 3. First mark the center of the Back with a *light* crease or pins. Pin the Stay to the *right* side of the Back, matching center lines.

With 12 stitches per inch (2.5 mm stitch length), begin sewing at one lower corner of the box. (Do not backstitch.) Sew on the stitching line across the bottom of the box. Then pivot and sew on the stitching line to the neck edge. Repeat for the other side, sewing across the bottom of the box a second time.

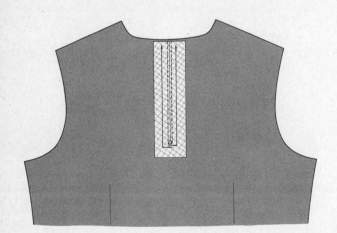

Now cut on the center line through both Stay and fabric. Cut into the corners of the box, forming a wedge. Be careful not to cut through the stitching.

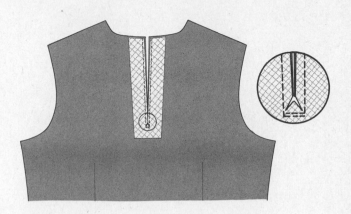

Turn the Stay to the wrong side and press the Stay and the seam allowances toward the center back as illustrated.

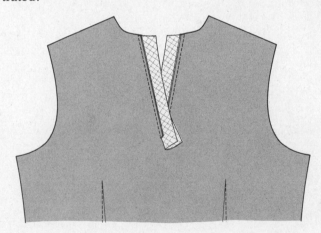

Shoulder Seams

Pin and stitch each shoulder seam, starting at the armhole and stitching toward the neck edge. Press the shoulder seams open and trim the seam allowances even with the neck edge.

Chanel Neckline Trim

With right sides together, place the Chanel strip even with the *cut edge of the Stay*. With the Chanel strip on top and the garment next to the sewing machine, stitch the Chanel strip to the neckline, using a ⅜-inch (1.0 cm) seam allowance. You should not stretch the neck edge of the garment, but stretch the strip slightly to eliminate the slack in the fabric. Trim the excess Chanel strip even with the cut edge of the Stay.

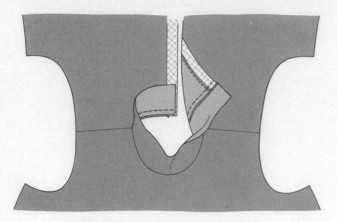

Press the Chanel strip and the seam allowances toward the neck opening.

Zipper Application

This application is basically the same as the zipper without a seam you learned in Class 3. The only difference is that in Class 3 the zipper was sandwiched between the layers of a turtleneck, but in your basic blouse the zipper is finished with the ends of the Chanel trim.

Turn the Stay and the ends of the Chanel strip to the wrong side to form a box for the zipper. The Stay should not be visible from the right side of the garment.

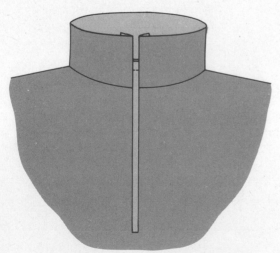

Apply basting tape to the right side of the zipper tape along the outside edges. Place the zipper in its finished position behind the box with the lower edge of the metal stop at the bottom of the box. The zipper teeth should be next to the edges of the box. The top of the

zipper pull should be ¼ inch (0.6 cm) into the Chanel strip. Finger-press the Stay to the basting tape on the zipper.

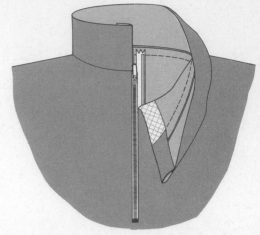

I suggest you use a zipper foot for sewing your zipper in place. Lift the Back as illustrated to expose the wedge at the bottom of the box. Stitch across the wedge through the Stay and the zipper tape.

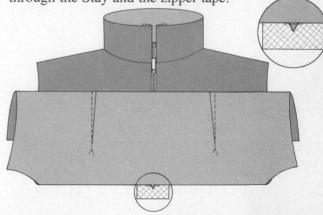

Fold the Back over as illustrated to expose the seam allowance along the side of the box. Beginning at the bottom of the box, sew next to the previous stitching, sewing on the garment side of the stitching line so the *Do-Sew* won't show from the right side. Stitch only to the cut edge of the neckline seam allowance.

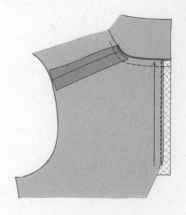

74

Sew the zipper to the other side of the Back in the same manner. Then remove the basting tape and trim the Stay and Chanel strip even with the edges of the zipper tape.

Unzip the zipper and turn the zipper tape toward the center back. At the top of the zipper, fold the ends of the zipper tape toward the seam allowance as illustrated. Do not cut them off because they will fray.

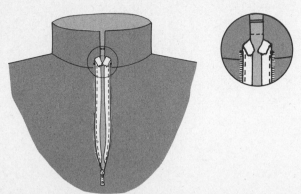

On each side of the zipper, fold the Chanel strip right sides together over the zipper tape. Stitch on the wrong side of the garment over the previous stitching line. Sew to ⅛ inch (0.3 cm) below the neckline seam as illustrated. Repeat for the other side of the zipper.

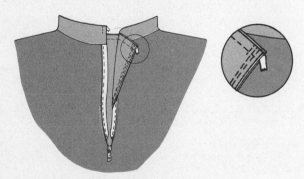

Turn the Chanel strip right side out.

Chanel Neckline Finish

Fold the Chanel strip over the seam allowances to the wrong side of the garment and pin it in place.

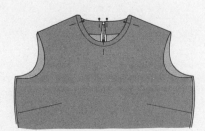

Stitch-in-the-ditch by sewing into the seamline on the right side of the garment. On the wrong side, trim the Chanel strip to ⅛ inch (0.3 cm) from the stitching. Press the trim and the neckline is complete.

Side Seams

Beginning at the lower edge of the blouse, pin and stitch each side seam.

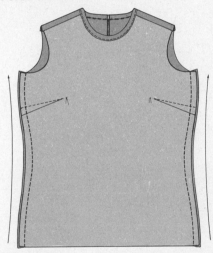

Press the seams open.

Armhole Finish

The armhole edges are finished by topstitching. You may use a regular needle for this or you may use a double needle. I enjoy topstitching with a double needle. The tiny ridge it creates on the surface of your garment is a feature you can use throughout your sewing — from mock tucks in the front of a blouse to stitched-in creases for the front of your pants. The double row of stitches is perfectly spaced automatically with no extra care on your part.

To topstitch the armholes, you should first machine baste around the armholes ⅜ inch (1.0 cm) from the edges. Press the armhole edges to the wrong side along the basting line. Then set your sewing machine at 6 stitches per inch (4 mm stitch length) and topstitch ¼ inch (0.6 cm) from the finished edges. Remove the basting stitches.

Hem

Press in a 1½-inch (3.8 cm) hem at the lower edge of the blouse. Bond or hand catchstitch the hem in place.

Give your blouse a final pressing and it's complete.

Special Information

Chanel-Trimmed Armholes

The armholes in the basic blouse may be finished with Chanel trim. If you decide to go this route, you will need to cut — in addition to the other garment pieces for the sleeveless blouse — two Chanel strips 2½ inches (6.4 cm) wide by 20 inches (50.8 cm) long.

Follow the instructions given previously for the basic blouse until you come to the heading, "Side Seams." Then follow the instructions below.

The procedure for applying Chanel trim to the armholes is very similar to the neckline application. First, cut away ⅜ inch (1.0 cm) from the armhole edges of

the blouse. This is the seam allowance provided for the topstitched armhole. A seam allowance is not required for a Chanel trim finish — the cut edge becomes the finished edge.

With right sides together, place a Chanel trim strip even with the underarm of the dress. With the strip on top and the garment next to the sewing machine, stitch the strip to the armhole with a ⅜-inch (1.0 cm) seam allowance. Stretch the strip slightly as you sew to eliminate the slack in the fabric. Trim the leftover strip even with the underarm, following the grain line in the fabric.

Press the Chanel strip and the seam allowances toward the armhole opening. Then, sew a strip to the other armhole in the same way.

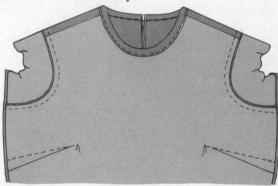

Pin and stitch each side seam, beginning at the lower edge of the blouse and sewing through the Chanel strip as illustrated. Remember to stretch as you sew. To reduce unnecessary bulk, trim the upper side seam allowances to ¼ inch (0.6 cm) as illustrated.

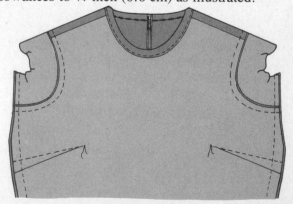

Fold the strip over the seam allowances to the wrong side of the garment and pin it in place. Secure the trim by stitching-in-the-ditch. On the wrong side, trim the excess Chanel trim to ⅛ inch (0.3 cm) from the stitching. Repeat for the second armhole.

Press in a 1½-inch (3.8 cm) hem at the lower edge of the blouse. Bond or hand catchstich the hem in place.

Adapting Chanel Trim

You have been introduced to the Chanel trim application while sewing your basic dress and blouse. This finish is as simple as it is attractive, and it has the advantage of being very versatile. You will find it in many *Stretch & Sew* patterns, including swimsuits, tops, and a variety of dresses.

What's even more exciting about Chanel trim is that you can adapt it to any pattern you choose. It makes a lovely hem finish for dresses and tops. Or, you can cut a scooped neck in a knit top pattern and trim the neckline just as you did for the basic dress. Any garment edge you would ordinarily finish with a hem, facing, or ribbing has the potential of being Chanel-trimmed if you know what you're doing. And now you do. Just remember these simple rules for applying Chanel trim to any cut edge:

1. Remember that a Chanel trim finish does not have the same stretch that a ribbing finish has. If a neckline won't slip over your head easily without stretching, you will need a zipper.

2. Select your fabric with the trim application in mind. Unless you apply Chanel trim along a straight edge, the fabric you are using for the trim must have some stretch, especially for a wider trim. If you are sewing a wide trim around a curved edge, the fabric should have at least 25 percent stretch. By the way, on curved edges I don't recommend trim wider than ½ inch (1.3 cm). If you are sewing a garment from a firm fabric, you may wish to apply a contrasting trim from a stretchier fabric such as ribbing or cotton interlock.

3. Cut away any seam allowance or hem allowance from the garment edge to which the trim will be applied. It's not required for a Chanel trim application because the cut edge of the fabric becomes the finished edge. The trim application doesn't subtract from the cut edge. In fact, approximately ⅛ inch (0.3 cm) is added where the trim folds over the cut edge.

4. Always cut your Chanel strip with the greater stretch running the length of the strip. The width of the strip should be approximately *five* times the desired width of the finished trim. For instance, the basic dress trim finishes at ½ inch (1.3 cm). So, you cut the Chanel strip five times that for a strip width of 2½ inches (6.4 cm). The length of the strip should be approximately the measurement of the edge you intend to finish.

5. Stitch the strip to the garment edge with a seam allowance ⅛ inch (0.3 cm) less than the desired width for the finished trim. For example, you stitched the strip to the basic dress with a ⅜-inch (1.0 cm) seam allowance and your finished trim was ½ inch (1.3 cm) wide.

Refer to these rules for applying Chanel trim whenever the creative mood strikes and you feel like doing your own fashion designing.

Notes

Chapter 5
Cardigan and Pullover Sweaters

Introduction

I would like to share some of my enthusiasm for sweater-sewing with you. I don't think there is any garment with the possible exception of a swimsuit that is more satisfying for me to sew than a sweater.

At Stretch & Sew, sweater fabrics coordinate with the solid and print fabrics in the various seasonal lines. You will not only be able to create a sweater quickly and easily, but you will also be able to complete a wonderful ensemble by selecting sweater fabric that coordinates with the other garments you have sewn for your classes. It will be truly rewarding when you sit back and take an overview of your labors. The fun of saying, "I made it," becomes greater and greater as time goes by.

As with all of the lovely fabrics that are carried in a *Stretch & Sew*® store, the sweater fabrics are carefully selected and tested to ensure you of fashion rightness, and quality continues to be of utmost importance. You will find our sweater fabrics among the most forgiving fabrics you will ever work with. They have great elasticity and mold into the proper shape with just a touch of steam.

Stretch & Sew® sweater patterns are designed with the utmost care — again with the right looks for your fashion needs. The ¼-inch (0.6 cm) seam allowances add to the ease of handling the fabric. You see, I share with you the concern for the time that goes into the development of any garment, and I never give it a second thought before I sew a sweater. I know that the time spent will be at a minimum, and the end result will be most satisfying. So join me in the fun of creating. Sew a sweater today!

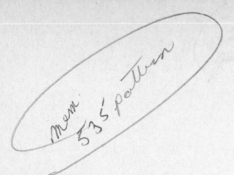

Cardigan and Pullover Sweaters

Pattern Selection

Stretch & Sew Pattern No. 635

The sweaters featured in Class 5 are from *Stretch & Sew* Pattern No. 635, Cardigan and Pullover Sweaters. You will be sewing a V-neck cardigan with a front button closing plus a pullover with a mitered rib trim finish for the V-neckline. Both sweaters have long sleeves stretched in just as you stretched sleeves into your T-shirt. The pattern also features crew neck and turtle-neck pullover sweaters.

Fabric Selection

Fabric for Your Cardigan and Pullover Sweaters

Sewing a sweater is as simple as sewing a T-shirt. And yet, many women are amazed to discover they can do it. In my years of teaching, I have found that their main concern is what will happen when they cut their sweater fabric. "Will my lovely fabric dissolve into a heap of runs and raveled yarn?" The answer is no.

Sweater fabric will ravel only when deliberate stress is applied. So, you will find cutting into your fabric and sewing your sweaters a fun and exciting experience. Of course, if you are working with a very loose, open sweater knit, you will want to handle the fabric with more care.

Cardigan and Pullover Sweaters Pattern No. 635 may be used with sweater fabric that has a finished edge. In this chapter I am featuring the construction of sweaters from this type of fabric. It is manufactured with rib knit along one edge of the fabric to provide a finished edge. You will cut your garment pieces with the lower edges

along the finished edge so that no hemming of the sweater is required.

The sweaters in this chapter may also be constructed from sweater yardage which does not have a finished edge. In this case, you would either hem your garment or you would finish the edges with matching rib trim. Instructions for both techniques are given under "Special Information" at the end of the chapter. The section on hemming describes the hand catchstitch which is the perfect stitch for those times when you choose to hem a knit garment by hand.

The cardigan is designed so that the front edges are finished with specially manufactured flat trim that matches its companion sweater fabric. The V-neckline of the pullover is constructed from specially manufactured matching rib trim. However, these trims are not necessary to sew the sweaters. Instead, you may use the sweater fabric itself. Instructions for these self-trim finishes are given under "Special Information" at the end of the chapter.

Both sweaters in this class are designed to be sewn in sweater fabric that has approximately 50 percent stretch. However, if you select a firmer fabric that has closer to 25 percent stretch, you should simply trace your pattern one size larger than usual.

Yardage and Notions

After you have selected your sweater fabric, refer to the back of the Pattern No. 635 envelope for yardage and notions. You will find that your *Stretch & Sew Fabrics*® center has a special line of color-coordinated *Stretch & Sew*™ buttons to help you achieve a truly ready-to-wear look in your cardigan. You will also need *Perky Bond*® fusible web to make sweater buttonholes as described in this chapter.

Cardigan Sweater with a Finished Edge

Preparing Your Pattern

Determining Your Pattern Size

Refer to the back of the Pattern No. 635 envelope and choose the size that corresponds to your bust measurement. Check the measurement charts to determine any necessary pattern adjustments.

Tracing Your Pattern Pieces

For your cardigan sweater, trace a View A Front, a View A Back, and a Sleeve. To trace whole pattern pieces, fold your tracing material and place the folded edge along each "Place on Fold" line on the master pattern.

Make any necessary pattern adjustments and transfer all pattern markings to your tracing material. The "Finished Edge" line on the pattern pieces is the cutting line for sweater fabric with a knit-on finished edge. The "Hemline" and the lower edge line are for sweater yardage that does not have a finished edge. Be sure to label these lines.

Cutting Your Fabric

Pretreating

Pretreat the sweater fabric and flat trim you have selected for your cardigan, following the care instructions which accompany the fabric.

Cutting Garment Pieces

From your sweater fabric with a finished edge, you will cut two View A Fronts, one View A Back, and two Sleeves. If you're cutting through one thickness at a time, remember to turn the Front pattern piece over to cut the second Front, so you will have a right side and a left side for your cardigan.

Fold each pattern piece along the "Finished Edge" line. Then place the pattern pieces on the sweater fabric so the "Finished Edge" lines are along the finished edge of the fabric.

You will notice that the knit-on rib draws up the fabric so that it doesn't lie flat along the finished edge. I handle this by cutting out the upper portion of each garment piece. Then I fold the pattern up approximately 4 inches (10.2 cm) above the finished edge and cut out the remaining garment piece by following the rib lines of the fabric. Continue cutting along the same rib lines through the finished edge.

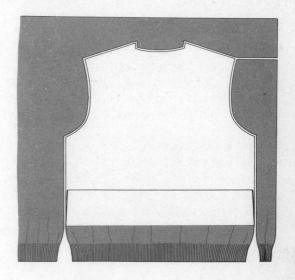

The flat trim for your cardigan will be cut during construction.

Sewing Your Cardigan Sweater

Unless otherwise indicated, stitch seams right sides together with a ¼-inch (0.6 cm) seam allowance. You will use a straight stitch with 9 stitches per inch (3 mm stitch length). By "right" and "left," I'm referring to the finished garment as if you were wearing it.

82

Raveling Yarn

In preparing to sew your cardigan, you will need to ravel some yarn for a small amount of hand stitching. You may ravel yarn from rib trim that matches your sweater fabric or you may take it from the sweater fabric itself.

In either case, pull out the end of a yarn from the side of the rib trim or sweater fabric opposite the finished edge and give it a firm pull. To remove the kinks from the yarn, draw the strand under a warm iron with plenty of steam. Apply very little pressure from the iron.

Shoulder Seams

In Chapter One you learned my rule that seams in knit garments must have elasticity for strength and in order to hang correctly. One exception to this rule is the shoulder seams of sweaters. Sweater fabric is so soft and stretchy that the shoulder seams should be stabilized or the weight of the Sleeves may cause them to droop.

There are two ways you can provide stability in these seams. One method is done by sewing machine and the other is done with a hand stitch. For either method, you should first pin and stitch the shoulder seams with a *⅝-inch (1.6 cm) seam allowance* and you should *not* stretch as you sew. Start at the armhole and sew toward the neckline.

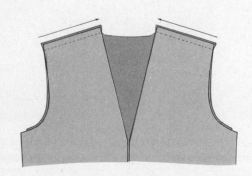

Next trim the Back seam allowances to ¼ inch (0.6 cm).

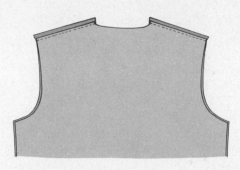

To finish the shoulder seams by sewing machine, fold both seam allowances toward the Back. Then topstitch ⅜ inch (1.0 cm) from the seam through all layers, using 6 stitches per inch (4 mm stitch length).

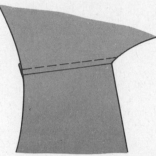

Finishing the shoulder seams with a hand stitch takes a little more care, but it gives the sweater a really rich look. Fold the Front seam allowance over and under the Back seam allowance. Using a single strand of raveled yarn, slipstitch the folded edge in place.

To slipstitch, take a very small stitch into the Back just under the fold, and then take a very small stitch into the fold itself. For clarity, the stitches in the illustration are shown above the fold. But you will want to take them just under the fold as I described so that your hand stitching will be invisible.

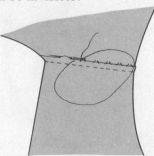

Sweater fabric requires little or no pressing. Instead, you should steam the shoulder seams without touching the iron to the fabric. Then finger-press the seams while the fabric is warm. Whenever you steam sweater fabric, allow it to cool before you move it and do not allow it to hang over the edge of the ironing board. The heat of steam relaxes the fibers of most sweater fabrics so that they will easily stretch out of shape while they are warm.

Sleeves

Applying Sleeves in your cardigan is just like applying them in a T-shirt. First fold the Sleeve in half and mark the center of the Sleeve cap with a pin.

Matching the pin to the shoulder seam, pin the Sleeve to the sweater armhole.

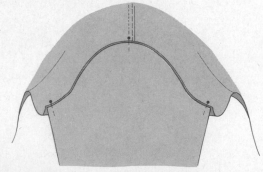

Next, with the garment on top and the Sleeve next to the sewing machine, sew the armhole seam with a ¼-inch (0.6 cm) seam allowance. Stretch the armhole slightly to match the Sleeve. Apply the second Sleeve in the same manner as the first.

Side Seams

You're on familiar ground as you sew the side seams. You will pin and stitch each side seam from the lower edge of the cardigan through the underarm to the lower

edge of the Sleeve. Be sure to match the edges of the knit-on ribs. When you sew seams in sweater fabric, sufficient stretching is usually accomplished by the pressure of the presser foot as the fabric feeds through the sewing machine.

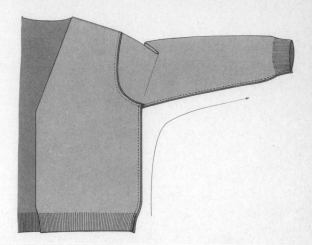

Flat Trim Application

Now you will apply flat trim to the unfinished edges of the cardigan. The first step is to determine the correct length of trim. The pattern is used for measuring because the garment itself will have relaxed to some degree as you were working with it. When you apply the trim, it will draw the sweater fabric back to its original shape along the cut edges.

Place your flat trim along the front edge of the Front pattern piece with the end of the trim even with the "Finished Edge" line. Use a pin to mark the trim ½ inch (1.3 cm) above the line. Place another pin at the point of the V-neckline as illustrated. Then place a third pin 1 inch (2.5 cm) below the shoulder edge.

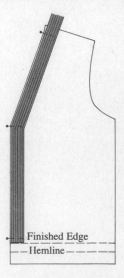

Finished Edge
— Hemline — — — —

Now continue on the neck edge of the Back pattern piece, positioning that third pin in your trim 1 inch (2.5 cm) below the shoulder edge. Mark the trim with a fourth pin at the center back.

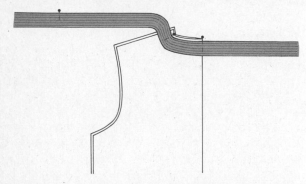

Fold the trim in half at the center back marking. Match pin markings as illustrated for the second half of the trim. Cut the trim ½ inch (1.3 cm) below the last pin.

Next fold the garment Back in half and mark the center back neck edge with a pin. Lapping the flat trim ½ inch (1.3 cm) over the cut edge of the cardigan, match the middle pin to the center back of the garment, the next pin to the shoulder seam, the next pin to the point of the V-neckline, and the last pin to the lower edge. Repeat for the second side of the cardigan. Then insert some additional pins to hold the flat trim in place.

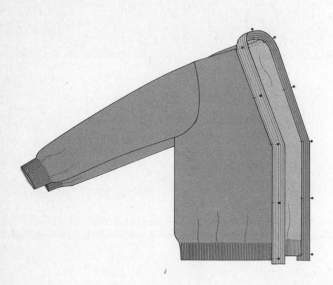

You will stitch ⅛ inch (0.3 cm) from the edge of the trim, pivoting at the points of the V-neckline. Ease the sweater in as you sew so that it matches the trim along the Front edges. To do this, sew with the trim on top and with the sweater fabric next to the sewing machine. Hold the sweater fabric so that it's relaxed as it feeds through the machine. Stretch the flat trim as necessary, especially across the Back neck edge to help the trim match the sweater.

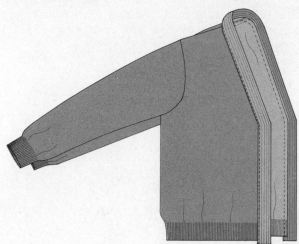

You will cut away part of the flat trim at the Back neckline so that it will curve comfortably when you wear the cardigan. First zigzag stitch along the center of the trim between shoulder seams as illustrated, stitching on the trim only.

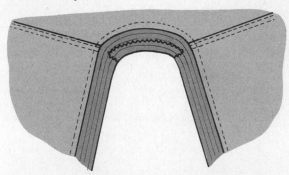

Now cut away the trim enclosed by the zigzag stitching.

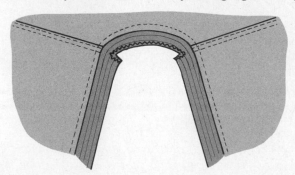

Fold the flat trim at the Back neckline to the wrong side of the garment. The edge of the trim should show on the right side. Using a single strand of your raveled yarn, whipstitch the trim to the sweater between shoulder seams. To whipstitch, catch the sweater fabric to the edge of the trim in each stitch.

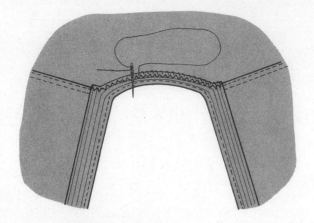

Turn the ½-inch (1.3 cm) extensions at the bottom of the sweater to the wrong side.

Then fold the trim in place along each Front edge of the sweater. At the lower edge, secure the trim with a whipstitch, but don't whipstitch along the entire Front edge. The buttonholes and buttons will keep the flat trim in position.

The lower edges of the garment are complete. No hemming will be necessary!

Buttonholes and Buttons

Now it's time to make your buttonholes. Many women are afraid to try this, but it's *not* difficult if you know a few little secrets. For instance, you should work your buttonholes from the trim side rather than from the right side of the garment.

Also, you should place a strip of *Perky Bond* on the trim where each buttonhole will be stitched. The *Perky Bond* makes it easier for the fabric to feed through your sewing machine as you stitch. After you complete the buttonholes, you will remove the excess *Perky Bond*. The *Perky Bond* that remains inside the stitches will stabilize the buttonholes so they will keep their shape. You will pin the *Perky Bond* in position—*do not* press it to the garment.

The first step in sewing your buttonholes is to sew a *practice* buttonhole. Place a strip of flat trim against a scrap of your sweater fabric. Use pins to mark the top and bottom of a vertical buttonhole. The cardigan is designed for ½-inch (13 mm) buttons, so we recommend ⅝-inch (1.6 cm) buttonholes. Secure a strip of *Perky Bond* as you pin.

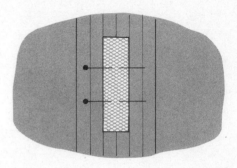

When you're sewing with knits and especially with sweater fabrics, you don't want to use a satin stitch for buttonholes. A satin stitch puts too much thread into a buttonhole and causes it to bubble out. Instead, you should set your machine at a loose zigzag stitch.

After you complete your practice buttonhole, examine it to make sure you're satisfied. If you have a good buttonhole, you are ready to sew buttonholes in your cardigan. Otherwise, try again on a sample until you are confident that you've mastered the technique.

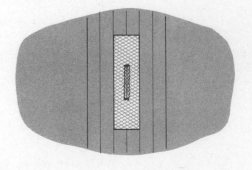

You will mark the buttonhole placement on the right Front of your cardigan. This is because, traditionally, women's garments button right over left and men's garments button left over right. I always tell women in my classes that it's easy to remember on which side to put buttonholes. Women are always right and men are left over!

Mark the buttonhole placement along the center front line, which is ⅝-inch (1.6 cm) from the flat trim stitching line. The top buttonhole should be at the point of the V-neckline and the bottom buttonhole should be in the center of the knit-on rib at the finished edge. Equally space the remaining three buttonholes. Pin strips of *Perky Bond* in place as you mark the buttonholes.

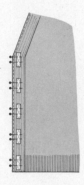

Stitch each buttonhole and pull away the excess *Perky Bond*. Use your iron to steam away any remaining *Perky Bond*. Be sure not to touch the iron to the fabric. Sew buttons in place on the left Front and you have completed your cardigan sweater.

Pullover Sweater with a Finished Edge

Preparing Your Pattern

Determining Your Pattern Size

Refer to the back of the Pattern No. 635 envelope and choose the size that corresponds to your bust measurement. Check the measurement charts to determine any necessary pattern adjustments.

Tracing Your Pattern Pieces

For your pullover sweater, trace a View C Back and a V-Neck Template. If you have not already traced the Sleeve for your cardigan sweater, trace it now to use for your pullover. To trace whole pattern pieces, fold your tracing material and place the folded edge along each "Place on Fold" line on the master pattern.

Make any necessary pattern adjustments and transfer all pattern markings to your tracing material. The "Finished Edge" line on the pattern pieces is the cutting line for sweater fabric with a knit-on finished edge. The "Hemline" and the lower edge line are for sweater yardage that does not have a finished edge. Be sure to label these lines.

Cutting Your Fabric

Pretreating

Pretreat the sweater fabric you have selected for your cardigan, following the care instructions which accompany the fabric. Do not pretreat the rib trim.

Cutting Garment Pieces

From your sweater fabric with a finished edge, you will cut two Backs (one to use as the Front) and two Sleeves.

Fold each pattern piece along the "Finished Edge" line. Then place the pattern pieces on the sweater fabric so the "Finished Edge" lines are along the finished edge of the fabric.

You will notice that the knit-on rib draws up the fabric so that it doesn't lie flat along the finished edge. I handle this by cutting out the upper portion of each garment piece. Then I fold the pattern up approximately 4 inches (10.2 cm) above the finished edge and cut out the remaining garment piece by following the rib lines of the fabric. Continue cutting along the same rib lines through the finished edge.

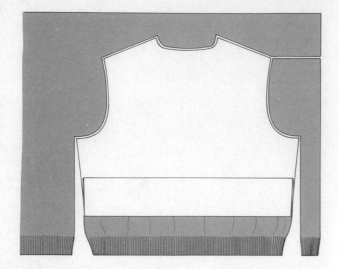

You will cut a V-neckline on one Back to use as the Front for your pullover. To do this, fold the Back in half along the center back line. Then pin the V-Neck Template to the Back as illustrated.

Using the Template as a guide, cut the V-neckline. Start cutting at the point of the V-neckline and cut to the shoulder edge.

The rib trim for your pullover will be cut during construction.

Sewing Your Pullover Sweater

Unless otherwise indicated, stitch seams right sides together with a ¼-inch (0.6 cm) seam allowance. You will use a straight stitch with 9 stitches per inch (3 mm stitch length). By "right" and "left," I'm referring to the finished garment as if you were wearing it.

Raveling Yarn

In preparing to sew your pullover, you will need to ravel some yarn for a small amount of hand stitching. Pull out the end of a yarn from the side of the rib trim opposite the finished edge and give it a firm pull. To remove the kinks from the yarn, draw the strand under a warm iron with plenty of steam. Apply very little pressure from the iron.

Shoulder Seams

First pin and stitch the shoulder seams with a ⅝-inch (1.6 cm) seam allowance. You should *not* stretch as you sew. Start at the armhole and sew toward the neckline.

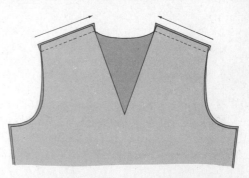

Next trim the Back seam allowance to ¼ inch (0.6 cm).

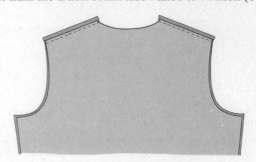

You may finish the shoulder seams by sewing machine or by hand stitching. To finish them by sewing machine, fold both seam allowances toward the Back. Then top-stitch ⅜ inch (1.0 cm) from the seam through all layers, using 6 stitches per inch (4 mm stitch length).

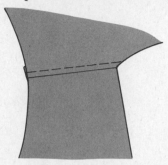

You may also finish the shoulder seams with a hand stitch. Fold the Front seam allowance over and under the Back seam allowance. Using a single strand of raveled yard, slipstitch the folded edge in place.

To slipstitch, take a very small stitch into the Back just under the fold, and then take a very small stitch into the fold itself. For clarity, the stitches in the illustration are shown above the fold. But you will want to take them just under the fold as I described so that your hand stitching will be invisible.

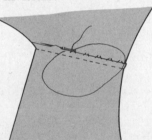

Sweater fabric requires little or no pressing. Instead, you should steam the shoulder seams without touching the iron to the fabric. Then finger-press the seams while the fabric is still warm. Whenever you steam sweater fabric, allow it to cool before you move it and do not allow it to hang over the edge of the ironing board. The heat of the steam relaxes the fibers of most sweater fabrics so that they will easily stretch out of shape while they are warm.

V-Neck Application

The V-neckline of your pullover is finished with rib trim which you will miter at the point of the V. Besides being fun to sew, this creates a very classic fashion look as well.

First cut a strip of rib trim to measure 1¼ inches (3.2 cm) wide *from the finished edge* by 27 inches (68.5 cm)

long. You can determine the finished edge of the trim because when you tug on it, the stitches won't pull apart.

Next measure the neckline of the Back *pattern piece* from the shoulder *seamline* — ⅝ inch (1.6 cm) from the shoulder edge — to the center back.

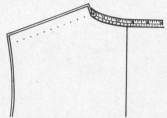

Determine two-thirds of this measurement. You may do this as you learned in Class 1. Fold the length of the measurement on the tape into thirds. Then unfold the last third and read the tape at the end of the second third. Add ¼ inch (0.6 cm) to the two-thirds measurement for seam allowance. Measure this length from one end of the rib trim and mark the trim with a pin.

cut. Trim wide

wide 2½ in 27 long

made v bigger cut long

Now mark the point of the V on the Front with a pin as illustrated.

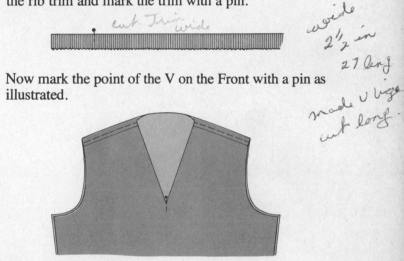

Then place the rib trim along the right side of the V-neckline, matching cut edges and matching the pin in the trim to the shoulder seam.

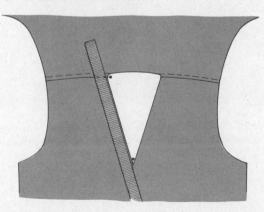

Using a ¼-inch (0.6 cm) seam allowance and slightly stretching the trim until you can see the ribs just begin to separate, stitch from the shoulder seam to the pin at the point of the V. Remove the pin and insert the sewing machine needle into the fabric exactly beneath the point of the V. Then pivot the garment and continue stitching to the left shoulder seam. Cut the remaining trim the same length as the first end.

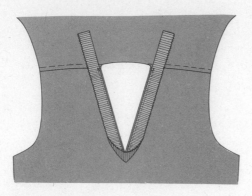

Sew the ends of the trim together and finger-press the seam allowances open. Then fold the pullover in half to find the center back. Match the seam in the trim to the center back of the neckline and pin. Finish sewing the neckline seam, stretching the trim to fit the Back neck edge.

At the center back, whipstitch the seam allowances to the trim as illustrated. To whipstitch, catch the trim to the edge of the seam allowance in each stitch.

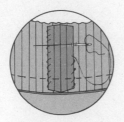

The only thing left to complete the V-neckline is to miter the rib trim at the point of the V. First clip the pullover Front to the point of the V, being careful not to cut through the stitching or the rib trim.

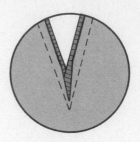

Fold the Front in half along the center front line with right sides together. Using your *Stretch & Sew*™ sewing gauge as a straightedge, mark a stitching line on the trim. Follow the center front line from the finished edge to the point of the V.

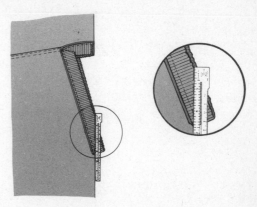

As you begin to sew, make sure the finished edges of the rib trim are even. Backstitch to the finished edges of the trim as illustrated. Then stitch along the line you have drawn to the point of the V.

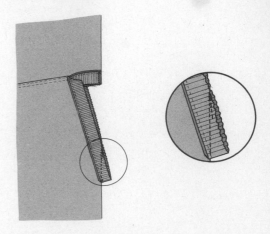

Now clip the rib trim to the point of the V, being careful not to cut through the stitching. Finger-press the seam in the trim open.

To secure the cut ends of the rib trim, fold the sweater out of the way and stitch them to the V-neck seam allowances, sewing over the previous stitching line. Take care not to catch the sweater Front in your stitching.

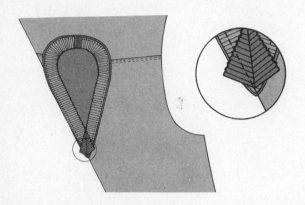

Cut the rib trim even with the seam allowances. Now the neckline is complete and you can take a moment to admire the lovely V-miter in your sweater.

Sleeves

First fold the Sleeve in half and mark the center of the Sleeve cap with a pin.

Matching the pin to the shoulder seam, pin the Sleeve to the sweater armhole.

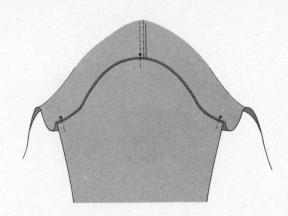

Next, with the garment on top and the Sleeve next to the sewing machine, sew the armhole seam with a ¼-inch (0.6 cm) seam allowance. Stretch the armhole slightly to match the Sleeve. Apply the second Sleeve in the same manner as the first.

Side Seams

You will pin and stitch each side seam from the lower edge of the pullover to the lower edge of the Sleeve. Be sure to match the edges of the knit-on ribs. When you sew seams in sweater fabric, sufficient stretching is usually accomplished by the pressure of the presser foot as the fabric feeds through the sewing machine.

Your pullover is complete and you've learned a really beautiful way to sew a miter in V-neckline trim. I consider it one of the easiest miters I've ever worked with. Now that you've learned the technique, you will want to sew pullover sweaters for the rest of your family.

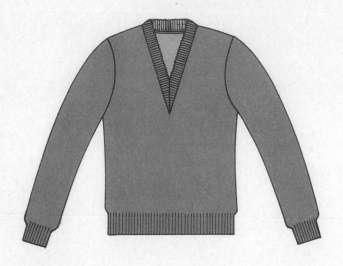

Special Information

Cardigan without Side Seams

For your cardigan it's possible to join pattern pieces to omit the side seams. I particularly like to do this when I am working with striped sweater fabric because there's just that much less matching to do when I cut the garment pieces and sew the cardigan.

To join the pattern pieces, trace two View A Fronts and one View A Back. Then lap them at each side seam ½ inch (1.3 cm), matching seamlines. Tape the pattern material in place.

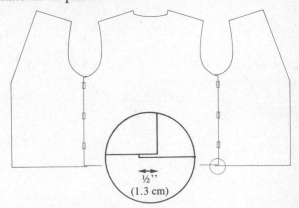

½"
(1.3 cm)

Cut one garment piece and two Sleeves from your sweater fabric. To sew the cardigan without side seams, refer to the instructions for the cardigan in the earlier part of this chapter. The only difference is that you will not have to sew side seams and the Sleeve application is as follows:

Sleeves

Beginning at the lower edge, pin and stitch each Sleeve seam.

Next mark the center of the Sleeve cap with a pin. Fold the garment in half at the shoulder seam, matching armhole edges. Mark the midpoint of the underarm with a pin.

Matching the pin in the Sleeve cap to the shoulder seam and matching the Sleeve seam to the underarm, pin the Sleeve to the garment armhole.

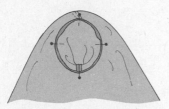

With the garment on top and the Sleeve next to the sewing machine, sew the armhole seam, stretching the armhole slightly to match the Sleeve. Apply the second Sleeve in the same manner as the first.

Cardigan with Self-Trim cut trim long way

It's possible to use your sweater fabric in place of flat trim to finish the front edges of the cardigan. Whenever you use your garment fabric for trim, it's called "self-trim."

For this application, you will need to cut two strips of sweater fabric 3 inches (7.6 cm) wide by 31 inches (78.7 cm) long with the greater stretch of the fabric running the width of each strip.

To splice the strips to make one long strip, place the ends right sides together at 90-degree angle and stitch as illustrated.

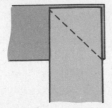

Trim the seam allowances to ¼ inch (0.6 cm) from your stitching and finger-press the seam open. Fold the strip in half lengthwise with right sides together. wrong.

Next use ¼-inch (0.6 cm) wide strips of *Perky Bond* fusible web to bond the cut edges of the folded fabric strip together. *Perky Bond* fuses sweater fabric with less heat than required for other fabrics. Don't actually press the fabric. Instead, use the steam of your iron to heat the *Perky Bond*. Then finger-press the edges of the fabric strip together while the *Perky Bond* is melted. Allow the fabric to cool before you move it from the ironing board.

Place the strip along the neck edge of the Back *pattern piece* with the middle of the miter at the center back. Place a pin in the strip at the center back. Then place a second pin 1 inch (2.5 cm) below the shoulder edge.

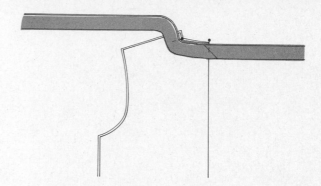

Continue measuring on the neckline of the Front pattern piece, positioning that second pin in your strip 1 inch (2.5 cm) below the shoulder edge. Mark the strip with a third pin at the point of the V-neckline. Then place a fourth pin ½ inch (1.3 cm) above the "Finished Edge" line if you are using fabric with a finished edge. For sweater yardage, which does not have a finished edge, place the fourth pin ½ inch (1.3 cm) above the "Hemline." Now cut the strip ½ inch (1.3 cm) below the last pin.

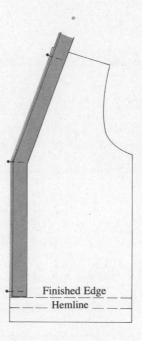

Fold the strip in half at the center back marking. Match pin markings for the second half of the trim and cut the trim ½ inch (1.3 cm) below the last pin.

Apply the self-trim to your cardigan just as you would apply flat trim. When you pin the trim to the sweater, the folded edge should face toward the side seams.

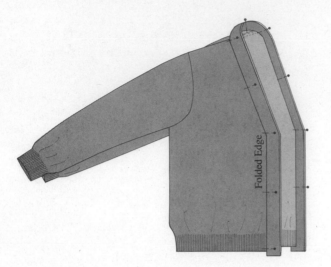

Pullover with Self-Trim

It's possible to use your sweater fabric in place of rib trim to finish the neckline of your pullover.

For this application, you will need to cut a strip of sweater fabric 2½ inches (6.4 cm) wide by 27 inches (68.5 cm) long with the greater stretch of the fabric running the length of the strip.

Fold the strip in half lengthwise and finger-press in a foldline. Then finish the V-neckline just as if you were using rib trim—except you should stretch the self-trim across the back neck edge with a 3:4 ratio rather than the 2:3 ratio described for the pullover in the earlier part of the chapter.

Cardigan or Pullover with Hemmed Lower Edge

In this chapter you learned how to sew cardigan and pullover sweaters using sweater fabric with a knit-on finished edge. It's also possible to sew these sweaters from sweater yardage, which does not have a finished edge. Refer to the back of the Pattern No. 635 envelope for fabric and notions required.

When you cut your fabric, use the lower edges of the pattern pieces for your cutting lines. Refer to the Suggested Cutting Layouts in the instructions for Pattern No. 635.

The reason you use the lower edge cutting line is to provide the necessary hem allowance for the sweater. Also, in the main garment pieces, there is extra length to create a longer finished garment measurement. A hemmed sweater requires a little more length for a flattering fit.

For the cardigan, follow the instructions in the earlier part of the chapter until you have sewn the side seams. *For the pullover,* follow the instructions in the earlier part of the chapter until you have constructed the entire garment. Then you will be ready to stitch the hems.

For each sweater, fold up a 1½-inch (3.8 cm) hem at the lower edge of the garment and a 1-inch (2.5 cm) hem at the lower edge of the Sleeves. Hand stitch the hems in place.

A hand stitch I recommend for hemming knits is the hand catchstitch. It's like a zigzag stitch done by hand. Since it provides stretch, you will have a stronger, smoother hem. This stitch has the additional advantage of keeping the cut edge of the hem allowance flat against the garment. To hem your sweater with a hand catchstitch, use a single strand of raveled yarn. Take tiny stitches into the hem allowance and then into the garment, working from left to right on the hem.

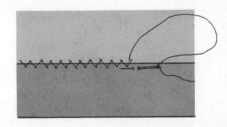

To complete your cardigan, begin measuring the flat trim on your Front pattern piece at the "Hemline" rather than at the "Finished Edge" line. Then continue with construction as usual. Stitch the bottom buttonhole approximately 1 inch (2.5 cm) above the lower edge of the sweater.

Cardigan or Pullover with Applied Rib Trim

If you purchase sweater yardage for your sweater as described above, you may wish to sew rib trim that has a finished edge to the garment lower edges rather than finishing them with hems.

For both sweaters, you will finish each Sleeve with rib trim 2¼ inches (5.7 cm) wide by your wrist measurement plus ½ inch (1.3 cm).

To finish the bottom *of the cardigan*, you will need rib trim 2¼ inches (5.7 cm) wide by three-fourths the measurement of the garment lower edge. To finish the bottom *of the pullover*, you will need rib trim 3 inches (7.6 cm) wide by your waist measurement minus 3 inches (7.6 cm).

Preparing Your Sleeve Pattern

For a cardigan or pullover, you will use your regular pattern pieces for the main part of the garment, but you will need to trace a new Sleeve pattern. Draw the lower edge cutting line ¾ inch (1.9 cm) above the "Finished Edge" line. Then extend the new lower edge 1 inch (2.5 cm) on the side. Connect the extensions to the underarm points as illustrated for a slightly wider Sleeve.

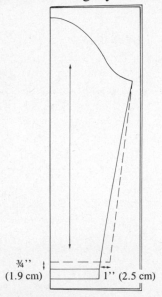

¾"
(1.9 cm)   1" (2.5 cm)

The reason you shorten the Sleeve is to compensate for the added length provided by the applied rib trim. The extra width creates an attractive blousing which is pulled in at the wrist by the stretched-on trim.

Cutting Your Fabric

For the cardigan, fold up the View A Front and the View A Back 1¾ inches (4.4 cm) above the "Finished Edge" line. This will shorten the pattern pieces to compensate for the added length provided by the applied rib trim. Cut two Fronts, one Back, and two Sleeves from your fabric. The rib trim will be cut during construction.

For the pullover, fold up the View C Back 2½ inches (6.4 cm) above the "Finished Edge" line. This will shorten the pattern piece to compensate for the added length provided by the applied rib trim. Cut two Backs and two Sleeves from your fabric. The rib trim will be cut during construction.

Sewing Your Sweater with Applied Rib Trim

For the cardigan, follow the instructions in the earlier part of the chapter until you have sewn the side seams. *For the pullover*, follow the instructions in the earlier part of the chapter until you have constructed the entire garment. Then you will be ready to apply rib trim to the garment lower edges.

You will apply rib trim to the Sleeves of the cardigan and the pullover in the same manner. Cut a strip of rib trim to measure 2¼ inches (5.7 cm) wide *from the finished edge* by your wrist measurement plus ½ inch (1.3 cm).

Sew the ends of the rib trim together, forming a circle. Finger-press the seam allowances open.

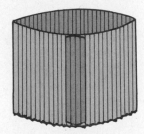

Divide the circle into fourths, marking the divisions with pins along the cut edge.

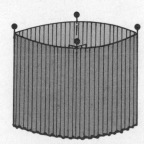

Next divide the Sleeve lower edge into fourths, marking the divisions with pins. Placing the seam of the rib trim at the Sleeve seam, pin the cut edge of the trim to the Sleeve edge, matching quarter divisions.

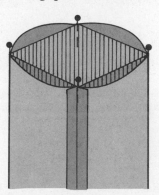

With the trim on top and the Sleeve next to the sewing machine, stitch, stretching the trim to match the Sleeve edge. Finish the second Sleeve lower edge in the same manner.

To finish the cardigan lower edge, cut a strip of rib trim to measure 2¼ inches (5.7 cm) wide *from the finished edge* by three-fourths the measurement of the garment lower edge.

Divide the strip into fourths, marking the divisions with pins along the cut edge. Then divide the garment lower edge into fourths, marking the divisions with pins. Pin the cut edge of the rib trim to the garment lower edge, matching quarter divisions.

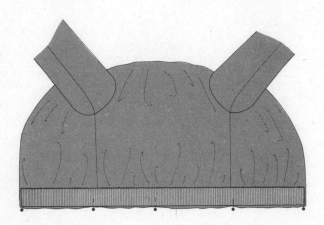

With the trim on top and the cardigan next to the sewing machine, stitch, stretching the trim to match the cardigan lower edge.

To complete your cardigan, continue with construction according to the instructions in the earlier part of the chapter. You will begin measuring the flat trim on your Front pattern piece at the "Finished Edge" line as described there.

To finish the pullover lower edge, cut a strip of rib trim 3 inches (7.6 cm) wide *from the finished edge* by your waist measurement minus 3 inches (7.6 cm). Apply the rib trim to the pullover lower edge in the same manner as you applied the rib trim to the Sleeve lower edges. Match the seam in the circle of rib trim to one of the side seams.

Cardigan or Pullover Vest

An exciting variation on the sweaters you've learned to sew for this class is the sweater vest. For either the cardigan vest or the pullover vest, rib trim with a finished edge is used to finish the armholes.

For each armhole you will need rib trim 1¼ inches (3.2 cm) wide by two-thirds the measurement of the garment armhole plus ½ inch (1.3 cm). The garment armhole will be larger than indicated by the pattern since you will be trimming the pattern armholes 1 inch (2.5 cm) to compensate for the width of the rib trim.

Preparing Your Pattern

For the cardigan, cut away 1 inch (2.5 cm) around the armholes of the View A Front and the View A Back.

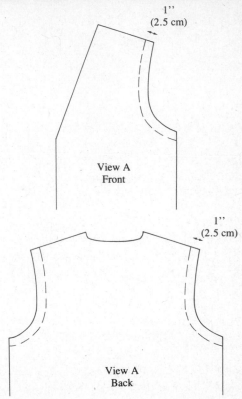

For the pullover, you should first straighten the side seam at the underarm of the View C Back. Measure in about ½ inch (1.3 cm) and taper into the side of the pattern piece as illustrated.

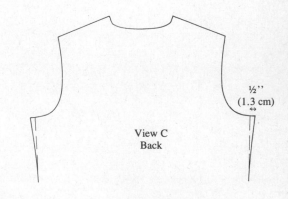

Then cut away 1 inch (2.5 cm) around the armholes.

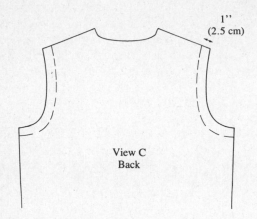

View C
Back

Cutting and Sewing Your Vest

Cut your fabric as described for the cardigan or pullover earlier in the chapter, using your adjusted pattern pieces. Of course, you won't need to cut Sleeves.

Sew your sweater as usual, omitting the Sleeve application. Finish the armhole edges after you have sewn the side seams. Rib trim is applied to the cardigan and the pullover in the same manner.

Cut a strip of rib trim to measure 1¼ inches (3.2 cm) wide *from the finished edge* by two-thirds the measurement of the armhole plus ½ inch (1.3 cm).

Sew the ends of the rib trim together, forming a circle. Finger-press the seam allowances open.

Divide the circle into fourths, marking the divisions with pins along the cut edge.

Next divide the armhole into fourths, marking the divisions with pins. Placing the seam of the rib trim at the underarm, pin the cut edge of the trim to the armhole, matching quarter divisions.

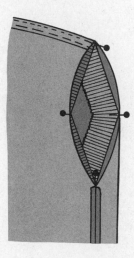

With the trim on top and the garment next to the sewing machine, stitch, stretching the trim to match the armhole. Finish the second armhole with rib trim in the same way.

Notes

Chapter 6
The Tab Front Dress

Introduction

The tab front is a classic fashion detail which adapts itself to many styles. For Class 6, we are featuring the tab front in a dress, but you will also find this type of neck opening in men's golf shirts and in sports shirts for women and for boys and girls of all ages.

The tab front has been a favorite with Stretch & Sew customers for many years. The technique I developed for applying the tab to the garment has consistently proven itself to be excellent. It eliminates a lot of room for error that exists in the many other ways it could be done. And, it's so much simpler!

You will find that applying the tab is in many ways similar to sewing the zipper without a seam which you learned earlier. Once again, you will be using *Do-Sew*® tracing material as a stay.

Sewing the tab front is the central technique you will learn in Class 6. Besides that, you will become familiar with *Perky Bond Plus*® fusible interfacing, a product which will save you hours of time and give your sewing the look of quality ready-to-wear. You will also learn how to construct and apply a collar which is designed with a fold going along the edge. This allows you to turn out the points more easily and ensures a more professional look to the finished collar.

The Tab Front Dress

Pattern Selection

Stretch & Sew® Pattern No. 1560

This class features a variation of *Stretch & Sew* Pattern No. 1560, View A. You will be sewing a tab front dress with a pointed collar, long sleeves with cuffs, and a tie belt.

View A of the pattern also has patch pockets with flaps, epaulets, and sleeve tabs for rolling up sleeves. These features have been omitted from the dress for your class to create a more classic style and to make it possible to focus on the construction and application of the tab and collar. However, there are some tips on interfacing and assembly-line topstitching under "Special Information" at the end of the chapter if you choose to add these optional items.

Pattern No. 1560 features a second dress with roll-up sleeves like the ones you sewed for your square neck raglan in Class 3. In addition, there is a classic tab front top and there is a top with a ribbing waist finish and cuffs. Both tops have a square collar.

Fabric Selection

Fabric for Your Tab Front Dress

I love choosing fabric for the tab front dress because there are so many looks you can achieve, depending on your fabric choice. I'm sure you will find fabric selection an exciting part of this class. A *Stretch & Sew Fabrics*® center is not just a place where you learn to sew but a place where you are encouraged to create fashion looks that truly are your own.

Make the tab and collar of the same fabric as the dress you are sewing or consider a contrasting fabric. An example might be a dark navy dress with red for the tab and collar.

Another idea for you to consider is using what are called "companion fabrics." These are fabrics designed to be used together — for instance, a large floral print that goes with a small floral print, or a stripe that goes with a plaid. In some cases a floral print will be designed to go with a stripe or a plaid. These fabrics can be used in the tab front dress to great advantage, creating a really distinct fashion look.

Yardage and Notions

After you have selected your fabric, refer to the back of the pattern envelope for fabric and *Perky Bond Plus* as indicated for View A. You will also need five ½-inch (13 mm) buttons and *Do-Sew* for the tab stay.

The Tab Front Dress

Preparing Your Pattern

Determining Your Pattern Size

Refer to the back of the Pattern No. 1560 envelope and choose the size that corresponds to your bust measurement. Refer to the measurement charts to determine any necessary pattern adjustments. Check center back length for all views because you will be preparing a multipurpose pattern.

Tracing Your Pattern Pieces

For your tab front dress, trace a Front, a Back, a Sleeve (with the curved lower edge), a Cuff, a Tab/Facing, a Pointed Collar, a Belt, and two Dress Adapters. You also need to trace a Tab Stay onto *Do-Sew* to use in the tab front application.

Make any necessary pattern adjustments and transfer all pattern markings to your tracing material.

101

Attaching the Adapters

By now you are familiar with the use of pattern adapters. Match one of the Dress Adapters to the placement line on the Front and secure it by stitching or taping right along the line. In the same manner, attach the other Dress Adapter to the Back.

Cutting Your Fabric

Pretreating

As usual, you will want to pretreat the fabric you have selected for your dress, following the care instructions which accompany the fabric. Do not pretreat *Perky Bond Plus*.

Cutting Garment Pieces

From your fabric, cut one Front, one Back, two Sleeves, two Cuffs, two Tab/Facings, one Pointed Collar, and one Belt. Depending on the width of your fabric, you may have to piece the Belt at the center. Follow the Suggested Cutting Layouts for View A in Pattern No. 1560, and remember to place the pattern pieces on the fabric so the greater stretch will go around the body in the finished garment. If you're cutting one thickness at a time, turn the pattern over to cut the second piece, so you will have a right side and left side for your dress. Transfer all construction marks to your fabric.

Pattern No. 1560 is designed to be used with a variety of fabrics, so it has ⅝-inch (1.6 cm) seam allowances. However, if you are working with cotton single knit, which rolls along the cut edge, you will find a ¼-inch (0.6 cm) seam allowance easier to work with when you set in the Sleeves. This is especially helpful if you are matching stripes. To establish a ¼-inch (0.6 cm) seam allowance, trim the armhole edges on the Front and the Back ⅜ inch (1.0 cm). Cut new notches as illustrated.

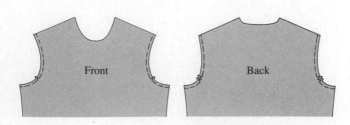

Then trim the upper edge of each Sleeve ⅜ inch (1.0 cm). Cut new notches.

Cutting Interfacing Pieces

From *Perky Bond Plus,* cut one Collar, placing the straight-of-grain line on the bias of the interfacing. You should also cut two Tab/Facings and two half Cuffs, cutting from the foldline of each Cuff to the cut edge. Place these pieces on the crosswise grain of the *Perky Bond Plus*.

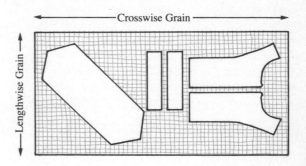

Trim the shoulder edge and the outside edge of each Tab/Facing interfacing ⅜ inch (1.0 cm) as illustrated.

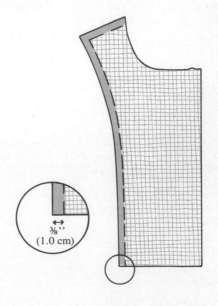

Sewing Your Tab Front Dress

Unless otherwise indicated, stitch seams right sides together with a ⅝-inch (1.6 cm) seam allowance. Use a straight stitch with 9 stitches per inch (3 mm stitch length) and stretch as you sew. For reinforcement, I recommend that you backstitch at the beginning and end of each seam. Remember that by "right" and "left," I am referring to the finished garment as if you were wearing it.

Interfacings

The first thing you will do is bond each *Perky Bond Plus* interfacing to the wrong side of its corresponding garment piece. The bonding process is very similar to the procedure you learned for *Perky Bond*® fusible web in Class 2.

Use a steam iron (wool setting) and a wet press cloth. I have found that white cotton interlock makes the perfect press cloth because it holds moisture so well. Take care as you press that the adhesive side of the *Perky Bond Plus* does not come in contact with your iron or your ironing board cover. For protection, place *Perky*® pattern paper between your ironing board cover and the garment pieces as you do your bonding. Then, if an interfacing piece is a bit larger than a garment piece, it will stick to the paper instead of your ironing board cover.

Press firmly in one place for 10 to 12 seconds or until the press cloth is dry. Do not slide the iron. Bond section by section, overlapping each time and rewetting the press cloth as necessary. After the fabric has cooled, lift one edge to check the bond. If the *Perky Bond Plus* pulls away from the fabric, repeat the procedure.

Remember, the steam from your iron and from the wet press cloth is essential to this process. The steam provides sufficient heat and carries the heat through the fabric to melt the beads of nylon on the *Perky Bond Plus,* fusing the interfacing with your garment piece. If you follow the procedure as described above, the bond should last the lifetime of your garment.

After you have bonded the interfacings, transfer all construction marks to your Tab/Facings. It's especially important to mark the center front lines to help you position the Collar correctly. You may simply indicate these lines at the neck edge, using your *Stretch & Sew*™ fabric marker.

Tab Stay

Now it's time to sew the Tab Stay to the Front. The Tab Stay provides a guide for your stitching and stabilizes the fabric while you sew. This beautiful method creates a smooth, professional-looking tab.

Fold the Front in half lengthwise and mark in the center front line with a *light* crease or pins. Pin the Tab Stay to the *wrong* side of the Front, matching the neck edges and the center front lines.

With 12 stitches per inch (2.5 mm stitch length), begin sewing at one lower corner of the box formed by the Stitching Lines. (Do not backstitch.) Sew on the Stitching Line across the bottom of the box. Then pivot and sew on the Stitching Line to the neck edge. Repeat for the other side, sewing across the bottom of the box a second time.

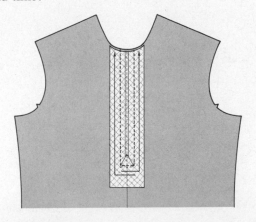

Cut on the Cutting Lines through both the Tab Stay and the fabric. Cut the point of the wedge as illustrated but, at this time, *do not* cut on the diagonal lines extending into the corners of the box.

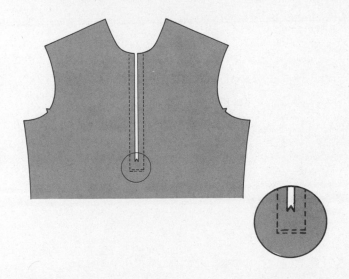

Tab Application

First, with right sides together, pin the Tab/Facings to the Front, matching cut edges.

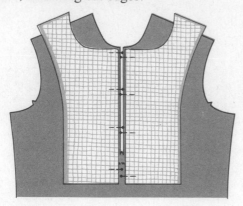

When you stitch the Tab/Facings in place, you will sew over the previous stitching on the Stay, but you will not sew across the bottom of the box yet. That comes later. On the wrong side of the Front, begin at the lower corner of the box and sew to the neck edge. Use your regular stitch length of 9 stitches per inch (3 mm stitch length). Repeat for the other side of the box.

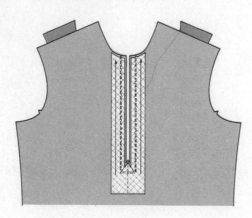

Place the Front on the ironing board to position the Tab/Facings. First, press each seam open.

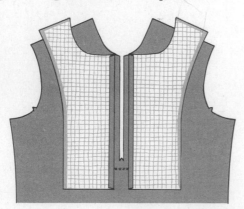

Then cut on the diagonal lines to the stitching at the corners of the box. Be careful not to cut through the stitching and cut only the Front and the Stay.

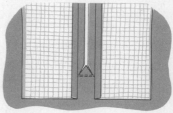

Next tuck the left Tab/Facing and the wedge at the bottom of the box to the wrong side. Fold the right Tab/Facing on the foldline and tuck it to the wrong side, filling the box as illustrated. Finger-press the right Tab in place, making sure it's even in width from top to bottom. The fold in the Tab should just match the edge of the box.

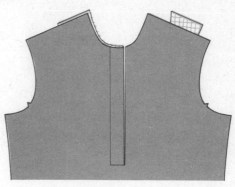

Fold down the left side of the Front and press the right Tab carefully.

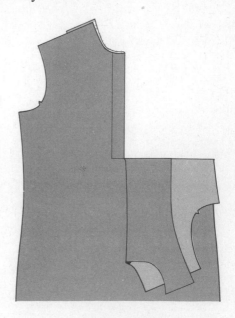

104

Reposition the left side of the Front. To keep the Tab secure while you stitch, tape it in place as illustrated, using transparent tape.

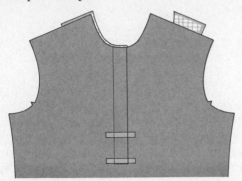

Lift the garment Front to expose the wedge and the right Tab/Facing at the bottom of the box. Machine baste across the wedge, sewing right over the previous stitching and sewing *toward the fold* of the Tab/Facing.

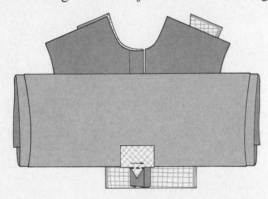

Now return to the ironing board and fold the left Tab/Facing on the foldline, positioning the left Tab under the right Tab. Then fold down the right side of the Front and press the left Tab carefully.

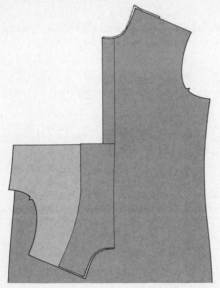

Lift the garment Front to expose the wedge and the Tab/Facings at the bottom of the box. With your usual 9 stitches per inch (3 mm stitch length), sew across the wedge, sewing over the previous stitching through all thicknesses.

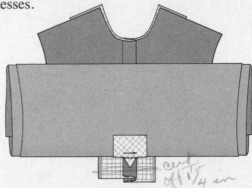

Trim the Tab Stay to ⅛ inch (0.3 cm) from your stitching and press the Tab carefully.

A topstitched "X-in-the-box" is a decorative detail often seen on tabs in ready-to-wear garments. I'll show you how to do it without removing the needle from the fabric.

Your box will be a 1-inch (2.5 cm) square set ⅛ inch (0.3 cm) from the sides and lower edge of the Tab. Mark the corners of the box with your *Stretch & Sew* fabric marker.

Set your sewing machine at 6 stitches per inch (4 mm stitch length) for topstitching. With the tab pinned in its finished position, start at the left upper corner and topstitch a square, pivoting at each corner. Don't backstitch and don't remove the needle from the fabric. Then, to complete the motif, follow the directional arrows as illustrated, sewing across the lower edge of the box a second time. Pull the threads through to the wrong side and tie them off.

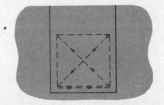

You may wish to trim the Facings on your dress. I take time to do this when, for instance, I have sewn a navy Tab in a white garment and the navy shows through.

First secure the Facings by stitching-in-the-ditch around the lower half of the Tab. Be careful not to catch the folded edges of the Tab in your stitching.

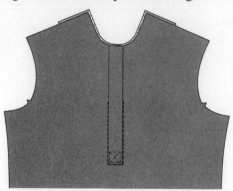

Then trim the Facings to approximately ¼ inch (0.6 cm) from the stitching. Continue trimming the Facings along the upper half of the Tab, tapering to full width at the shoulders. The illustration clearly shows how much to trim.

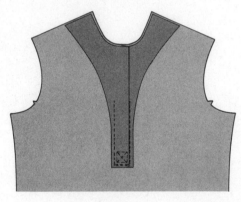

Take a moment to enjoy the satisfaction of completing your Tab. Going step by step and using the Stay to guide your stitches, it wasn't hard at all. You'll have your tab front dress finished before you know it.

Shoulder Seams

Pin and stitch each shoulder seam, starting at the arm-hole and stitching toward the neck edge. Be careful not to catch the Tab/Facings in your stitching. Press the shoulder seams open.

Collar Construction

This Collar is a joy because it's so simple to sew and yet so attractive. As you construct and apply the Collar,

notice my tips on directional stitching, trimming, and pressing. Following these tips will take no time at all and they will make a great deal of difference in your finished Collar.

First fold the Collar on the foldline with right sides together. Pin and stitch the ends, sewing toward the fold.

Next trim the Collar seam allowances to ¼ inch (0.6 cm) and clip the corners as illustrated.

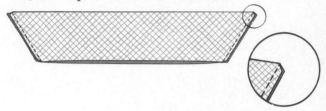

To keep the seams from rolling to the inside when you turn the Collar, take a moment to press them open as illustrated.

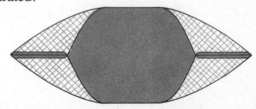

Turn the Collar right side out. Then work the fabric with your fingers to bring the points out as far as possible. The next step is to insert a *Stretch & Sew*™ point turner into the Collar and gently push the remaining fabric out into nice smooth points. I am very careful when I work with the point turner that I don't push too hard because it's possible to work the point turner right through the fabric.

The next step is to press the Collar, allowing the seams to roll slightly to the underside as you press. Then they won't show from the right side of the Collar.

Now, using a straight stitch with 6 stitches per inch (4 mm stitch length), topstitch ⅛ inch (0.3 cm) from the finished edges, pivoting at the corners. Topstitch a second row ¼ inch (0.6 cm) from the first row.

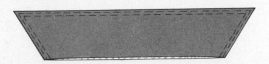

Collar Application

Fold the Collar in half and mark the center back neck edge with a pin. Repeat for the garment Back. Place the under Collar against the right side of the garment, matching center backs and matching the ends of the Collar to the *center front* on each Tab. Pin the Collar in place along the neck edge and along the center of each Tab as illustrated. Pinning the ends of the Collar keeps them in place while you stitch so the finished Collar will lie symmetrically.

Machine baste the Collar to the neck edge, sewing from the center front to the center back on each side of the neckline. (Do not include the Facings in this stitching.) Sewing the Collar directionally in this way also helps the finished Collar lie symmetrically.

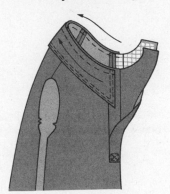

Fold each Tab/Facing along the foldline with the right side of the Facing against the right side of the Collar. Match cut edges at the neckline and match center front markings. Each foldline should be ⅝ inch (1.6 cm) from the end of the Collar. Pin the Facings in place.

Next stitch the neckline, sewing from the front edge to the center back on each side of the dress. Do not stretch this seam as you sew.

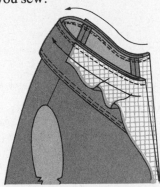

Grade the neckline seam allowances to varying widths, leaving the seam allowance of the upper Collar full width along the Back neck edge. Along the Front neck edge, leave the Facing seam allowance widest.

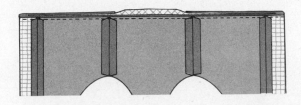

Turn the Facings to their finished position and press. Press the neckline seam allowances toward the garment. To secure the Facings, stitch-in-the-ditch by sewing into the shoulder seamline on the right side of the garment from the neck edge to the end of the Facings.

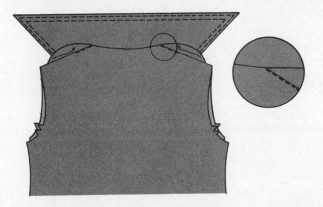

Stitch the neckline seam allowance to the dress along the Back neck edge ¼ inch (0.6 cm) from the seamline. Trim the seam allowance to ⅛ inch (0.3 cm) from the stitching.

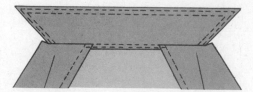

Now you've learned the basics of collar construction and application. These techniques will ensure a quality ready-to-wear look in the tab fronts you sew for yourself and for your family. And when you sew your jacket for Class 7, you'll find that you've already mastered the Collar.

Side Seams

Beginning at the lower edge of the dress, pin and stitch each side seam. Press the side seams open.

Sleeve Construction

Fold a Sleeve right sides together at the slash, matching cut edges. Beginning ½ inch (1.3 cm) above the slash, stitch down 1 inch (2.5 cm), using a ¼-inch (0.6 cm) seam allowance.

If you are setting in the Sleeves with a ⅝-inch (1.6 cm) seam allowance and if your fabric has little vertical stretch, you will need to gather the Sleeve cap to ease it into the armhole. Machine baste two rows of gathering stitches ½ inch (1.3 cm) and ¾ inch (1.9 cm) from the edge of the Sleeve cap between the notches.

Next pin and stitch the Sleeve seam, beginning at the lower edge. Press the seam open. Then machine baste two rows of gathering stitches ½ inch (1.3 cm) and ¾ inch (1.9 cm) from the lower edge of the Sleeve between the notches.

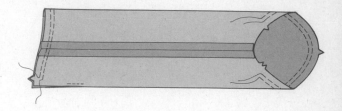

Sew the second Sleeve in the same manner as the first.

Cuffs

Constructing the Cuffs is very similar to constructing the Collar. First fold a Cuff on the foldline with right sides together. Pin and stitch the ends, sewing toward the fold. Next trim the Cuff seam allowances to ¼ inch (0.6 cm).

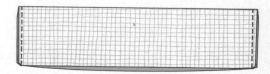

To keep the seams from rolling to the inside when you turn the Cuff, press them open. Then turn the Cuff right side out and work out the corners with your point turner. Press the Cuff, rolling the seams slightly to the underside. The interfaced side of the Cuff is the outer Cuff.

Using a straight stitch with 6 stitches per inch (4 mm stitch length), topstitch ⅛ inch (0.3 cm) from the finished edges, pivoting at the corners. Topstitch a second row ¼ inch (0.6 cm) from the first row.

Matching the ends of the Cuff to the notches at the slash, pin the Cuff to the Sleeve with the outer Cuff (interfaced side) next to the right side of the Sleeve. At the notches, fold the edges of the slash over the ends of the Cuff and pin. Then pull the bobbin threads of the basting stitches, gathering the Sleeve to fit the Cuff. Adjust the gathers evenly. Next stitch the Cuff to the Sleeve through all thicknesses and remove the basting stitches.

Construct and apply the second Cuff in the same manner as the first.

Sleeve Application

Pin the Sleeve to its armhole, matching Front and Back notches and matching the notch on the Sleeve cap to the shoulder seam. If you gathered the Sleeve cap, pull slightly on the bobbin threads of the basting stitches to ease the fullness of the Sleeve cap to fit the armhole. Then with the Sleeve on top and the garment next to the sewing machine, stitch the Sleeve to the armhole. If you did not gather the Sleeve cap, stitch with the garment on top and the Sleeve next to the sewing machine. Stretch the garment fabric slightly and allow the teeth in the machine to ease the Sleeve cap into the armhole.

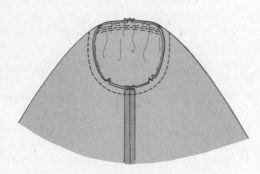

Doublestitch by sewing a second row of stitching on the seam allowance ⅛ inch (0.3 cm) from the previous stitching. Remove the basting stitches from the Sleeve cap and trim the seam allowances ⅛ inch (0.3 cm) from the second row of stitching.

Next, with the Sleeve on top and the garment next to the ironing board, steam the seam allowances as illustrated.

This will ease the fullness of the Sleeve, providing a smooth seam.

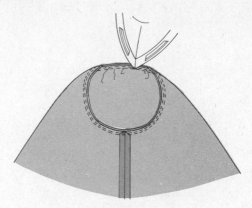

Set in the second Sleeve in the same manner as the first.

Hem

Your tab front dress has a 2-inch (5.1 cm) hem allowance. Try on the dress to check the length. Then press the hem in place and secure it by bonding with *Perky Bond* or by using a hand catchstitch.

Belt

Here are general instructions for constructing the Belt for the tab front dress. As you sew the Belt, you may wish to refer to Chapter Three to review the technique for turning it with cording.

Fold the Belt in half lengthwise. Then pin and stitch the length of the Belt with a ¼-inch (0.6 cm) seam allowance. With the seam in the center of the Belt as illustrated, press the seam open.

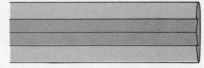

Turn the Belt right side out. Press the Belt again with the seam in the center. Fold the cut edges to the inside of the Belt. Bond with *Perky Bond* or hand stitch to finish the ends of the Belt.

Next, using a straight stitch with 6 stitches per inch (4 mm stitch length), topstitch ⅛ inch (0.3 cm) from the finished edges, pivoting at the corners. Topstitch a second row ¼ inch (0.6 cm) from the first row.

Buttonholes and Buttons

Machine stitch three vertical ⅝-inch (1.6 cm) buttonholes along the center front of the right Tab. Begin the top buttonhole ½ inch (1.3 cm) below the neck edge of the Tab, and end the bottom buttonhole ½ inch (1.3 cm) above the topstitching on the lower edge of the Tab. Center the middle buttonhole between the top and bottom buttonholes.

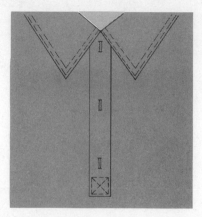

Machine stitch buttonholes on the Cuffs, following the buttonhole placement markings from the pattern. Then sew ½-inch (13 mm) buttons in place on the left Tab and on the Cuffs.

Press your tab front dress and it's ready to wear! You'll want to share the excitement with the rest of the family — make tab fronts for them, too. Now that you've learned the basic techniques, you may wish to try some of the variations under "Special Information" which follows. You'll certainly want to take advantage of the tab front's versatility by sewing it in a variety of fabrics.

Special Information

How to Lengthen the Tab

If you wish to lengthen the Tab for fashion effect, it's very simple. The finished Tab in Pattern No. 1560 is 9½ inches (24.1 cm) long. Determine how much longer you wish your Tab to be. Then draw a line across the center of the Tab Stay. Cut on the line and lengthen the pattern piece the desired amount. Back the opening with your tracing material, taping it in place. Reconnect the lines on the Stay. Lengthen the Tab/Facing pattern piece at the lower edge by the same amount you lengthened the Tab/Stay.

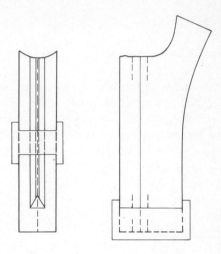

Trace your adjusted Tab Stay onto fresh *Do-Sew* to use as your Stay while sewing.

When you start sewing, follow the instructions just as if you hadn't lengthened the pattern pieces. Easy, isn't it? I sometimes lengthen the Tab to below the waist for a shirtwaist dress look.

The Basic Dress with Tab and Collar

Some women, especially those who are large-busted, feel more comfortable wearing a dress with a bust dart — even when the dress is made from knit fabric which provides wearing ease. If you are one of these women, you may simply apply the Tab/Facings and the Collar from Tab Front Dress and Top Pattern No. 1560 to the basic dress from the Basic Dress and Blouse Pattern No. 1505. The necklines of the two patterns are identical, making it possible to interchange pattern pieces in this way.

Sleeves from Pattern No. 1560 may also be sewn into the basic dress. However, the Sleeve notches will not exactly match the notches on the Front and Back. Set each Sleeve in as usual, matching underarm seams and matching the notch on the Sleeve cap to the shoulder seam. Begin easing the Sleeve cap to the armhole when your stitching reaches the notch on the Sleeve.

Interfacing Options

For most fabrics, interfacing both the upper and under halves of the Collar and interfacing the complete Tab/Facing works very well. For heavyweight fabrics or for sweater fabrics, there are some other options.

Interfacing Heavyweight Fabrics

For heavyweight fabrics, you may wish to reduce the amount of interfacing. To do this, cut only half a Collar from *Perky Bond Plus*, cutting from the foldline of the Collar to the cut edge. Treat the interfaced side of the Collar as the *upper* Collar during construction. Also, you should interface only the Facing part of the Tab/Facing, using the foldline for the dividing line as illustrated.

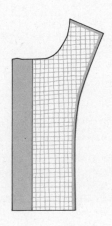

Interfacing Sweater Fabrics

For sweater fabrics, it's necessary to provide body to the Tab and Collar by interfacing them. At the same time you will wish to retain the soft appearance of the fabric. To do this, cut only half a Collar from *Perky Bond Plus*. Treat the interfaced side of the Collar as the *under* Collar during construction.

Since the top button of the Tab is customarily left unbuttoned and the Facing folds out at the neckline, you want the Facing to have the same soft appearance as the

upper Collar. To achieve this look, interface only the Tab part of the Tab/Facing, using the foldline for the dividing line as illustrated.

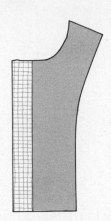

Bonding before Cutting Interfacings

Whenever I am sewing a garment which requires many small pieces to be interfaced, I save a lot of time by bonding *Perky Bond Plus* to part of my fabric first. Then I cut out my garment pieces — already interfaced! A good occasion for following this procedure would be when you are sewing View A from the Tab Front Dress and Top Pattern No. 1560. This dress has Pocket Flaps, Epaulets, and Sleeve Tabs, all of which may be cut from previously bonded fabric.

Since most interfacing pieces are cut with the straight-of-grain line running along the crosswise grain of the *Perky Bond Plus*, bond the interfacing to your fabric with the crosswise grain running along the lengthwise grain as illustrated. Then you can cut nearly all interfaced pieces from the bonded fabric.

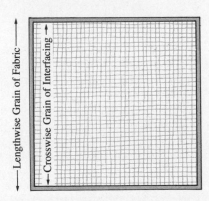

Some interfacings must be cut and bonded in the regular manner. These include partial interfacings like half Cuffs and interfacings cut on the bias like Collars.

111

Raised or Recessed Tab

Generally, when I construct a tab front garment, I sew the Tab/Facings to the Front and then I press the seams open. This distributes the seam allowances evenly and creates a Tab that is flush with the surrounding garment. However, I sometimes vary this look. To do this, apply the Tab Stay and sew the Tab/Facings to the Front in the usual manner. When it's time to place the garment on the ironing board to arrange and press the Tab/Facings, I press the seam allowances according to the desired effect as follows.

For a *raised* Tab, press both seam allowances *toward* the center front and keep them in that position as you complete the Tab. The double layer of seam allowances will fill out the edges of the Tab, causing the Tab to stand out from the garment.

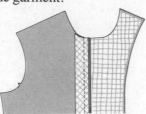

For a *recessed* Tab, press both seam allowances *away from* the center front and keep them in that position as you complete the Tab. The double layer of seam allowances will fill out the garment around the Tab, causing the Tab to appear slightly recessed compared to the garment.

Assembly-Line Topstitching

I would like to give you some tips to speed up your sewing when there are several pieces which must be constructed and topstitched before you apply them to the garment. A good example is the tab front dress, especially if you are adding Pockets, Epaulets, and Sleeve Tabs as featured in View A of Pattern No. 1560. But these tips apply even to the simpler version of the dress presented in this chapter.

A word of caution — make sure you understand how a garment will go together before you follow my suggestions. As always, you should read through the instructions before you begin sewing.

First of all, I like to topstitch as many pieces as possible all at once. Then I don't have to remember to adjust my stitch length regulator back and forth from a standard stitch length to the longer stitch length used for topstitching. And, if I'm using contrasting thread for a decorative effect, it's even more desirable to complete most of the topstitching in one step. Then you can avoid rethreading your sewing machine again and again.

If you were sewing View A of Pattern No. 1560, for instance, you would find that the Pocket Flaps, the Collar, the Epaulets and Sleeve Tabs, the Cuffs and the Belt can all be constructed and then topstitched before you put the dress together.

When I topstitch a series of garment pieces, I use what I call the "home base" technique to eliminate the fuss and bother of a bunch of loose threads. For your home base, use a rectangle of fabric which is stabilized with *Perky Bond Plus*. The following illustration, which shows an Epaulet from Pattern No. 1560, will demonstrate the technique. Notice that adjacent rows of topstitching always go in the same direction.

Place the garment piece flush with the edge of the home base, being careful not to overlap them. Start your topstitching on the home base. Then stitch directly onto the garment piece. When you finish a row of topstitching, sew from the garment piece back onto the home base. Then sew across the home base to stitch the second row as illustrated.

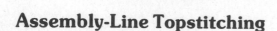

Leaving the needle inserted in the home base, cut threads to release the garment piece. Now sew from the home base onto the next garment piece to be topstitched. Continue until all the desired pieces have been topstitched.

Topstitching Options

The double row of topstitching on your tab front dress is an optional decorative feature which is especially attractive in a solid-colored garment. When you are sewing with printed fabric, you may wish to use a single row of topstitching ¼ inch (0.6 cm) from the garment edges. Or, you may wish to omit topstitching altogether. The choice is yours — it simply depends on your desired finished look.

Chapter 7
Classic Jacket and Straight Skirt

Introduction

You'll find the classic jacket a great addition to your wardrobe. The design is simple and yet versatile. The cut-on facing, the machine-made buttonholes and the patch pockets add to the simplicity of the jacket without taking away from its good looks.

You have already mastered many of the construction techniques for the jacket. You learned the sleeve application when you sewed your basic dress and you learned how to construct and apply a collar for your tab front. Sewing the jacket will give you an opportunity to build your confidence and polish your techniques.

The straight skirt is a flattering skirt which is always an important part of the fashion scene. The encased elastic waistband in the skirt is a technique you'll find yourself using over and over again for other skirts and for pants. It offers the simplicity of a pull-on waist finish along with the elegant appearance of a conventional waistband.

Classic Jacket and Straight Skirt

Pattern Selection

Stretch & Sew® Pattern No. 1040

The jackets featured in *Stretch & Sew* Pattern No. 1040 have bust darts and patch pockets. View A, which you will be sewing for Class 7, is a basic jacket with a square collar and long sleeves. View B of Pattern No. 1040 is more tailored in its construction with back panels, a vent and an optional belt across the back. View C has short sleeves, back waistline darts, and a V-neck without a collar. As you can see, there are a great many ways in which this pattern can be sewn and used in your wardrobe.

Stretch & Sew Pattern No. 445

In Class 7 you will sew View A of *Stretch & Sew* Pattern No. 445. View A is a straight skirt with a center back pleat. Pattern No. 445 features several other skirt styles, including dirndl skirts with continental or side seam pockets and street-length or floor-length A-line skirts. All of these skirts feature the encased elastic waistband technique you'll be learning in Class 7. And, they are all handsome worn with the classic jacket.

Fabric Selection

Fabric for the Jacket and Skirt

The jacket and skirt are attractive sewn in a wide variety of fabrics. Your choice of fabric will determine whether they take on a sportive appearance or a softer, more elegant appearance. If you want to achieve a traditional suit look, select a fabric with a firm enough hand to create the desired effect. Also, it's important that the fabric for your skirt have at least 25 percent stretch. Then the waistband will be able to stretch comfortably over the hips.

Many of you will want to sew your jacket from the same fabric you sewed your pants in for Class 2.

Another idea for you to consider is sewing a second jacket and a skirt from plaid fabric. There are layouts under "Special Information" at the end of this chapter to help you perfect your plaid-matching techniques. If your pants and skirt from Class 2 are from solid-colored fabric, select a plaid that coordinates with that color. Then you will be able to mix and match your plaid pieces with your solid pieces.

In Chapter Four I took time to discuss print fabrics. Now I would like to give you some information about jacquards. Jacquards are fabrics in which the design is knitted in rather than printed on. These fabrics are made on very special, very elaborate knitting machines. It's likely that the plaid you select for your jacket and skirt will be a jacquard.

The jacquard machine may create the design in a fabric by working with different colored yarns. Or a yarn of one color may be knit into a raised and lowered surface pattern to form the design. Occasionally, yarns of different fibers are knit into the fabric, and a design becomes apparent after the fabric is dyed because each yarn accepts the dye differently.

In jacquards, colors carried across on the back of the fabric may affect the colors on the surface. This is called "grin-through." Because of grin-through, I recommend that you select coordinate fabrics from the less dominant colors of a jacquard. Then a slight difference in shading will not be apparent.

Yardage and Notions

After you have selected your fabric, refer to the back of the pattern envelopes for yardage and notions. Pattern No. 445 requires *Stretch & Sew*™ 1-inch (2.5 cm) elastic. This is a woven elastic which is firmer than the narrower, braided elastic you used for the turned-down elastic finish in Class 2. *Stretch & Sew* woven elastics are used in waistbands. These elastics will never roll in the waistband casing and they keep their strength even after you stitch through them.

The Classic Jacket

Preparing Your Pattern

Determining Your Pattern Size

Refer to the back of the Pattern No. 1040 envelope and choose the size that corresponds to your bust measurement. Check the measurement charts to determine any necessary pattern adjustments.

Tracing Your Pattern Pieces

For your classic jacket, you will need to trace a Front, a Back, a Sleeve, a Collar, an Upper Pocket, and a Lower Pocket.

The bust dart in Pattern No. 1040 provides the same fit as the bust dart in the Basic Dress and Blouse Pattern No. 1505. In other words, if you found it necessary to lengthen, shorten, raise, or lower the dart when you prepared your basic dress pattern for Class 4, you will need to make the same adjustment for your jacket bust dart. If you need to refresh your memory, refer to the section "Bust Dart Adjustment" in Chapter Four. There you will find the Standard High Point Measurements Chart as well as complete instructions for making an adjustment.

If you found that no bust dart adjustment was necessary when you prepared your basic dress pattern, the dart for your size in Pattern No. 1040 will fit your figure. The dart drawn on the pattern is for size 30 only. To draw in the dart for other sizes, mark the dot given for your size. Then draw lines from the dot to the corresponding notches on the side of the pattern.

The back waistline darts are not featured in View A of Pattern No. 1040, but I recommend that you trace them on your Back pattern piece now for future use. These darts have been drawn for size 30 only. If you are a different size, mark the dots for your size. Then shift the tracing material, aligning the traced dots to the size 30 dots on the master pattern. Trace the dart.

Make any necessary pattern adjustments and transfer all pattern markings to your tracing material. If you raised or lowered the dart, raise or lower the top buttonhole placement marking the same amount. Check to make sure the middle buttonhole placement marking is exactly halfway between the top and the bottom placement markings.

Cutting Your Fabric

Pretreating

Pretreat the fabric you have selected for your jacket, following the care instructions which accompany the fabric. Do not pretreat *Perky Bond Plus®* fusible interfacing.

Cutting Garment Pieces

If you are working with plaid fabric, refer to the information under "Special Information" at the end of the chapter before you actually cut into your fabric. The layout provided there will help you to match plaids in your jacket.

From your fabric, you will need to cut two Fronts, one Back, two Sleeves, one Collar, one Upper Pocket and two Lower Pockets.

Follow the Suggested Cutting Layouts for View A in Pattern No. 1040, and remember to place the pattern pieces on the fabric so the greater stretch will go around the body in the finished garment. If you're cutting one thickness at a time, turn the pattern over to cut the second piece so you will have a right and left side for your jacket.

Transfer all construction marks to your fabric. It's especially important to mark the center front lines on the Fronts to help you position the Collar correctly. You may simply indicate these lines at the neck edge, using your *Stretch & Sew™* fabric marker.

Cutting Interfacing Pieces

From *Perky Bond Plus,* cut one Collar, placing the straight-of-grain line on the bias of the interfacing. You should also cut two Front facings, cutting from the foldline on the Front to the edge of the facings. For these pieces, place the foldline along the crosswise grain of the *Perky Bond Plus*. Finally, cut one Upper Pocket and two Lower Pockets on the crosswise grain, cutting along the interfacing lines indicated on the pattern pieces.

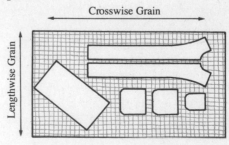

Transfer all construction marks to the interfacings. Then trim the shoulder edge and the outside edge of each Front facing interfacing ⅜ inch (1.0 cm) as illustrated.

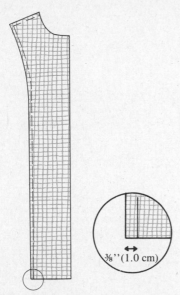

⅜"(1.0 cm)

Sewing Your Jacket

Unless otherwise indicated, stitch seams right sides together with a ⅝-inch (1.6 cm) seam allowance. You will use a straight stitch with 9 stitches per inch (3 mm stitch length) and stretch as you sew. For reinforcement, I recommend that you backstitch at the beginning and end of each seam. Remember that by "right" and "left," I am referring to the finished garment as if you were wearing it.

Interfacings

The first thing you will do is bond each *Perky Bond Plus* interfacing to the wrong side of its corresponding garment piece. As you learned in Class 6, you will use a steam iron (wool setting) and a wet press cloth, preferably white cotton interlock. Take care as you press that the adhesive side of the *Perky Bond Plus* comes in contact only with the fabric — not with your iron or ironing board cover. For protection, place *Perky®* pattern paper between your ironing board cover and the garment pieces as you do your bonding.

Press firmly in one place for 10 to 12 seconds or until the press cloth is dry. Do not slide the iron. Bond section by section, overlapping each time and rewetting the press cloth as necessary. After the fabric has cooled, lift one edge to check the bond. If the *Perky Bond Plus* pulls away from the fabric, repeat the procedure.

Darts

Fold each bust dart along the center and pin. Sew the darts, starting at the notches and stitching in a straight line to the point. Then tie off the threads at the point of each dart. Press the darts down.

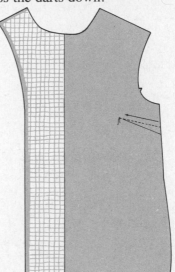

Pockets

Next you will construct and apply patch pockets to the jacket Fronts. I will be describing a special technique for easing the fullness of the seam allowance to the inside for a smooth curve when you topstitch each pocket in place.

Fold one Lower Pocket right sides together along the foldline to create a facing for the upper edge. Then stitch with a ⅝-inch (1.6 cm) seam allowance from the fold to the edge of the facing on each side. Trim the facing to ⅜ inch (1.0 cm) from the stitching as illustrated.

Beginning and ending at the facing, machine baste around the Pocket exactly ⅝ inch (1.6 cm) from the edge.

Next machine baste around the lower curves of the Pocket ¼ inch (0.6 cm) from the edge.

Turn the facing to its finished position, rolling the seams slightly to the underside. Then bond the facing to the Pocket with *Perky Bond*® fusible web.

Using the machine basting as a guide, press ⅝ inch (1.6 cm) to the wrong side along the edge of the Pocket. Pull the bobbin threads of the second line of machine basting to gather the lower Pocket curves as illustrated.

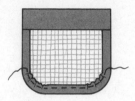

Now trim the lower Pocket curves close to the second line of machine basting as illustrated.

Matching the upper corners of the Pocket to the pocket placement dots, pin the Pocket to the right Front. Or, instead of pinning, you may wish to use ¼-inch (0.6 cm) strips of *Perky Bond* to secure the Pockets. Slip the strips under the side and lower edges and bond the Pocket to the Front. This technique is excellent for holding the Pocket in position while you are topstitching. I especially recommend using *Perky Bond* when you are matching plaids. A little secret I'll let you in on is that sometimes I've bonded pockets to a garment and never bothered to topstitch them at all. The *Perky Bond* was sufficient to hold the pockets in place.

Using a straight stitch with 6 stitches per inch (4 mm stitch length), topstitch the Pocket in place ⅛ inch

(0.3 cm) from the edge. Topstitch a second row ¼ inch (0.6 cm) from the first row. Remove the basting stitches.

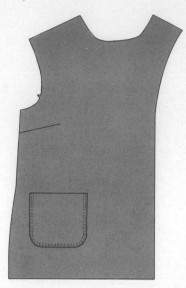

Construct the remaining Lower Pocket and the Upper Pocket and apply them to the left Front just as you constructed and applied the first Lower Pocket.

Shoulder Seams

Pin and stitch each shoulder seam, starting at the armhole and stitching toward the neck edge. Press these seams open.

Collar Construction

You will find that the construction and application of the collar for your jacket are basically the same as for your tab front collar in Class 6. This will give you an opportunity to practice so that applying a collar according to the *Ann Person*™ sewing method becomes second nature.

Fold the Collar with right sides together along the foldline. Pin and stitch the ends, sewing toward the fold.

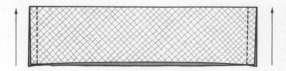

Trim the seam allowances to ⅜ inch (1.0 cm) from the stitching. To provide a crisp finish when you turn the Collar, take a moment to press the seams open. Then

turn the Collar right side out. Use a *Stretch & Sew*™ point turner to make sure the corners of the Collar are nice and sharp. Press the Collar, rolling the seams to the underside.

Using a straight stitch with 6 stitches per inch (4 mm stitch length), topstitch ¼ inch (0.6 cm) from the finished edges of the Collar.

Collar Application

Fold the Front wrong sides together along the facing foldline. Press in a crease along the foldline.

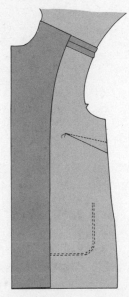

Now fold the Collar in half and mark the center back neck edge with a pin. Repeat for the garment Back. Place the underside of the Collar against the right side of the garment, matching center backs and matching the ends of the Collar to the *center front* on each side. Pin the Collar in place along the neck edge and along the center fronts as illustrated.

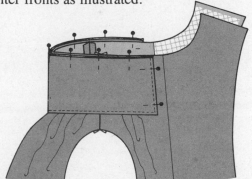

Machine baste the Collar to the neck edge, from the center front to the center back on each side the neckline. Do not include the facings in this stitching.

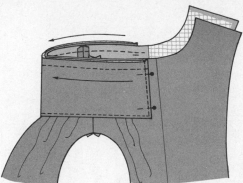

Fold each facing along the foldline with the right side of the facing against the right side of the Collar. Match cut edges at the neckline and match center front markings. Each facing foldline should be ¾ inch (1.9 cm) from the end of the Collar. This provides an overlap along the front of the jacket for buttons and buttonholes. Pin the facings in place.

Stitch the neckline, sewing from the front edge to the center back on each side of the jacket. Do not stretch this seam as you sew.

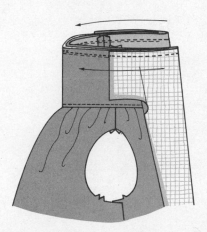

Next grade the neckline seam allowances to varying widths, leaving the seam allowance of the upper Collar full width along the Back neck edge. Along the Front neck edge, leave the facing seam allowance widest.

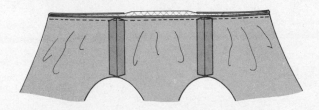

119

Turn the facings to their finished position and press. Press the neckline seam allowances toward the garment. To secure the facings, stitch-in-the-ditch by sewing into shoulder seamline on the right side of the jacket from the neck edge to the end of the facings.

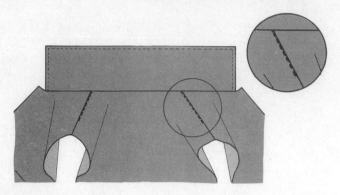

Stitch the neckline seam allowance to the jacket along the Back neck edge ⅜ inch (1.0 cm) from the seamline. Trim the seam allowance to ⅛ inch (0.3 cm) from the stitching.

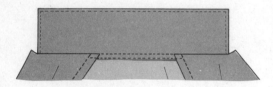

Side Seams

Beginning at the lower edge of the jacket, pin and stitch each side seam.

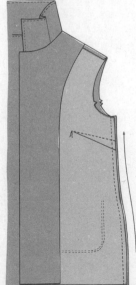

Press the seams open.

Sleeves

The Sleeve cap must be gathered to fit into the armhole of the jacket. One way to gather the Sleeve cap is by following the technique you learned for the Sleeve in the basic dress.

Machine baste two rows of gathering stitches ½ inch (1.3 cm) and ¾ inch (1.9 cm) from the edge of the Sleeve cap between the notches.

Another way to gather the Sleeve cap is the "ease-plus" technique. It is simpler and quicker once you've tried it a few times. With your regular 9 stitches per inch (3 mm stitch length), stitch right along the seamline between the notches. *As you stitch*, place a forefinger on either side of the presser foot and push the fabric through faster than it would feed by itself. The fabric will gather up along the seamline.

Next pin and stitch the Sleeve seam, beginning at the lower edge. Press the seam open.

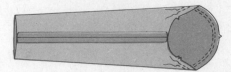

Pin the Sleeve to its armhole, matching Front and Back notches and matching the notch on the Sleeve cap to the shoulder seam. If you gathered the Sleeve cap according to the first method, pull slightly on the bobbin threads of the basting stitches to ease the fullness of the Sleeve cap to fit the armhole. If you ease-plussed the Sleeve cap and find that it's gathered too much, clip the stitches every few inches to relax the seamline. If it's not gathered enough, use a pin to pull at the stitches, drawing up the Sleeve cap to fit the armhole.

With the Sleeve on top and the garment next to the sewing machine, stitch the Sleeve to the armhole.

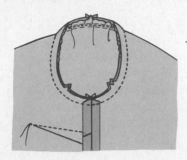

Doublestitch by sewing a second row of stitching on the seam allowance ⅛ inch (0.3 cm) from the previous stitching. Remove the basting stitches from the Sleeve cap and trim the seam allowances ⅛ inch (0.3 cm) from the second row of stitching.

Next, with the Sleeve on top and the garment next to the ironing board, steam the seam allowances as illustrated. This will ease the fullness of the Sleeve, providing a smooth seam.

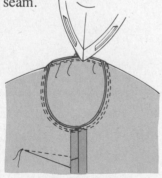

If you have a pressing ham, I suggest you also steam the Sleeve from the right side. Place the ham in the armhole where it will fill out the jacket as your own shoulder would. Then, with the seam allowances toward the Sleeve, steam the seam once again. Don't actually touch the iron to the seam because you don't want to flatten it. That would spoil the roll of the Sleeve cap.

Set in the second Sleeve in the same manner as the first.

Hems

Press in a 1-inch (2.5 cm) hem at the lower edge of each Sleeve. Bond or hand catchstitch the Sleeve hems in place.

Fold each facing along the foldline right sides together with the Front. Stitch across the facing along the 2-inch (5.1 cm) hemline.

Trim the facing hem allowance to ⅜ inch (1.0 cm) from the stitching as illustrated.

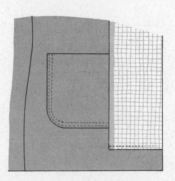

Turn the facings to their finished position. Then press in a 2-inch (5.1 cm) hem at the lower edge of the jacket. Bond or hand catchstitch the hem in place.

Buttonholes and Buttons

Machine stitch horizontal buttonholes on the right Front, following the buttonhole placement markings. Sew ¾-inch (19 mm) buttons in place on the left Front. The buttons should be stitched along the center front line — ¾ inch (1.9 cm) from the front edge.

¾''
(1.9 cm)

The buttons and buttonholes hold the facings to the Front along the folded edges. You may secure the cut edges of the facings by "spot-bonding" with pieces of *Perky Bond* behind the lapels and the Lower Pockets. The lapels and Pockets will keep the points of attachment from being noticeable from the right side of the jacket. If your fabric has enough body, the bonding may not be noticeable and you can use ¼-inch (0.6 cm) strips of *Perky Bond* along the entire length of the facings next to the edges. I recommend that you test this first on scraps of your fabric to make sure it doesn't show.

Press your jacket, tuck a handkerchief into the breast pocket, and you're nearly ready to go. First you'll want to sew a matching straight skirt according to the following instructions.

The Straight Skirt

Preparing Your Pattern

Determining Your Pattern Size

Refer to the back of the Pattern No. 445 envelope and choose the size that corresponds to your hip measurement. Check the measurement charts to determine any necessary adjustments. Remember that the skirt must pull up over the hips. It's best not to trace down more than one size at the waist. Instead, rely on the elastic to draw in the waistline of the skirt.

Tracing Your Pattern Pieces

For your skirt, trace one Straight Skirt Front, placing the fold of your pattern material along the "Place on Fold" line. Trace one Straight Skirt Back, tracing along the "Cutting Line for Back." You will also need to trace a Waistband.

Make any necessary pattern adjustments and transfer all pattern markings to your tracing material. If you lengthen or shorten the skirt, do *not* change the placement of the dot that marks the center back pleat.

Cutting Your Fabric

Pretreating

Pretreat the fabric you have selected for your skirt, following the care instructions which accompany the fabric. Do not pretreat the elastic.

Cutting Garment Pieces

If you are working with plaid fabric, refer to the information under "Special Information" at the end of the chapter before you actually cut into your fabric. The layout provided there will help you match plaids in your skirt.

From your fabric you will need to cut one Front, two Backs, and one Waistband. Follow the Suggested Cutting Layouts for View A in Pattern No. 445, and remember to place the pattern pieces on the fabric so the greater stretch will go around the body in the finished garment. If you're cutting one thickness at a time, turn the Back pattern piece over to cut the second piece so you will have a right and left side to the back of your skirt. Transfer all construction marks to your fabric.

You will also need to cut a strip of *Stretch & Sew* 1-inch (2.5 cm) elastic equal to your body waist measurement.

Sewing Your Skirt

Unless otherwise indicated, stitch seams right sides together with a ⅝-inch (1.6 cm) seam allowance. You will use a straight stitch with 9 stitches per inch (3 mm stitch length) and stretch as you sew. For reinforcement, I recommend that you backstitch at the beginning and end of each seam. Remember that by ''right'' and ''left,'' I'm referring to the finished garment as if you were wearing it.

Darts

Fold each Front dart along the center and pin. Sew the darts, starting at the notches and stitching in a straight line to the point. Then tie off each dart at the point. Press the darts toward the center of the garment.

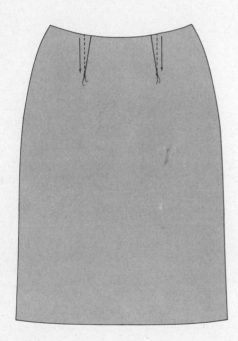

In the same manner, sew the dart in each Back.

Back Seam

Beginning at the lower edge, pin and stitch the Backs together. Do not press this seam open.

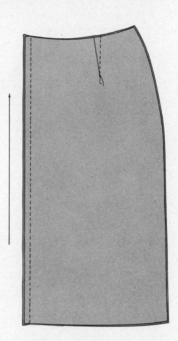

Backstitching securely at the dot, sew along the ''Stitching Line for Vent'' from the dot to the waist edge.

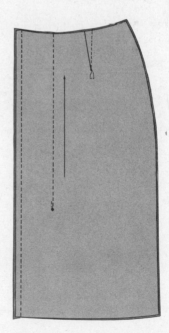

Press the pleat toward the left. Then machine baste the pleat in place ½ inch (1.3 cm) from the waist edge.

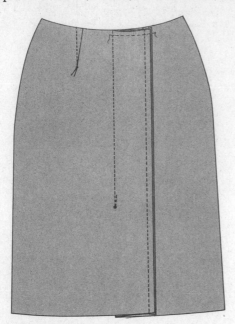

Side Seams

Beginning at the lower edge, pin and stitch each side seam.

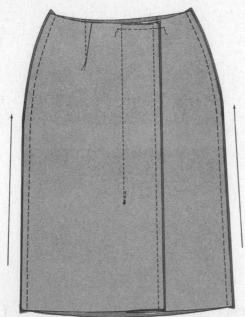

Press the side seams open.

Now that the seams are sewn, some of you may wish to trim the back waist edge of the skirt. This will apply to those of you who found it necessary to trim the four-gore skirt for Class 2. If you trimmed that skirt, trim the back waist edge of the straight skirt the same amount.

Encased Elastic Waistband

The technique for the encased elastic waistband is one of the primary techniques you will be learning during your class series. This waistband looks the same as a conventional waistband that must be accompanied by a zipper. But, actually, it's a pull-on waist finish that takes you hardly any time at all to sew.

If you have not already cut your elastic, cut a strip of *Stretch & Sew* 1-inch (2.5 cm) elastic equal to your body waist measurement. Lap the ends of the elastic ½ inch (1.3 cm), forming a circle, and stitch securely. Divide the elastic into fourths and mark the divisions with pins.

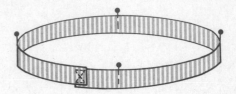

Pin and stitch the ends of the Waistband. Then press the seam open.

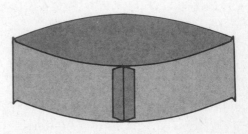

Pin the Waistband to the skirt, matching the notches to the side seams and matching center fronts and center backs. Stitch, firmly stretching both the Waistband and the skirt.

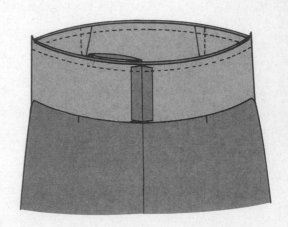

Pin the elastic to the wrong side of the Waistband seam allowance, matching quarter divisions to the side seams, the center front and the center back.

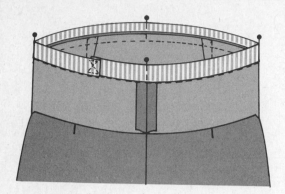

With the elastic on top and the skirt next to the sewing machine, zigzag the elastic to the skirt seam allowances. Stretch the elastic to fit the skirt, keeping the lower edge of the elastic next to the Waistband seamline.

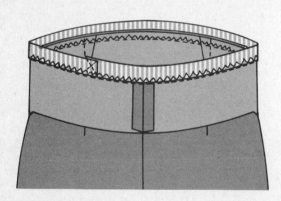

If you are using a straight stitch, sew the elastic to the waist seam allowances, firmly stretching all layers.

Fold the Waistband tightly over the elastic to the wrong side of the skirt and pin it in place as illustrated.

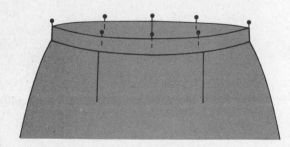

To finish the Waistband, stitch-in-the-ditch by sewing into the seamline on the right side of the skirt, stretching the elastic until the Waistband is straight and taut. Catch the Waistband in your stitching on the wrong side of the skirt.

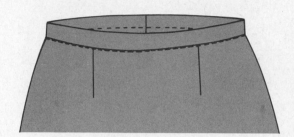

Trim the Waistband seam allowance ¼ inch (0.6 cm) from the stitching and the waist application is complete.

Hem

Clip into the seam allowance of the pleat 4 inches (10.2 cm) above the lower edge of the skirt. Take care not to cut through the stitching.

Next trim the seam allowance below the clip to ¼ inch (0.6 cm). Then press it open.

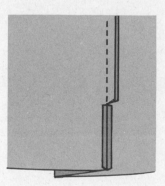

Press in a 2-inch (5.1 cm) hem at the lower edge of the skirt. Next fold the skirt right sides together at the pleat seamline and pin.

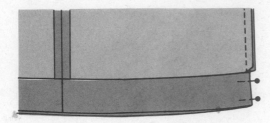

Using a ¼-inch (0.6 cm) seam allowance, stitch through all thicknesses from the lower edge to the top of the hem allowance, joining the previous stitching.

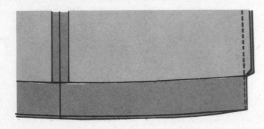

Bond or hand catchstitch the hem in place. Then give your skirt a final pressing, taking special care to create a sharp-looking center back pleat.

Special Information

Matching Plaids in the Jacket

When you cut plaid fabric for your classic jacket, match the center back line of the Back to a dominant vertical stripe in the plaid design. Then match the middle of the Collar to the same vertical stripe.

Cut one Front, matching the center front line along a dominant vertical stripe. You should also match horizontal stripes to the Back along the side seamline from the lower edge of the Front to the lower dart notch. Flip this Front over to cut the second Front, matching stripes.

Match the straight-of-grain line on the Sleeve to a dominant vertical stripe. Since the Fronts and Back do not match at the underarm because of the dart, you cannot match the Sleeve to both the Fronts and the Back at the underarm. You should match the horizontal stripe at the front underarm point of the Sleeve to the underarm point of the Fronts. Then the horizontal stripes at the armhole will match when seen from the front. Flip this Sleeve over to cut the second Sleeve, matching stripes.

The Pockets may be cut so they blend into the plaid design when you sew them to the jacket. To do this, use the "Cutting Lines for Interfacing" on the Pocket pattern pieces when you do your matching. These will become the finished edges on the actual Pockets. Using the pocket placement dots on the Front as a guide, draw pockets (finished size) on the Front pattern piece. Cut the Pockets from your fabric so that they exactly match the plaid where you have drawn in pockets on the Front.

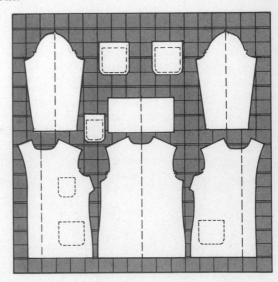

Another option for cutting the Pockets from plaid fabric is to cut them on the bias. First establish a bias line as described in Chapter Two under the heading, "Chevroned Stripes in the Four-Gore Skirt." Then cut the Pocket pieces on the diagonal by placing the bias line along a stripe. Be sure to flip the first Lower Pocket over to use as a pattern for cutting the second Lower Pocket, matching stripes.

Matching Plaids in the Skirt

When cutting plaid fabric for your straight skirt, place the center front line of the Front pattern piece along a dominant vertical stripe in the plaid design. Match the center front line of the Waistband piece to the same stripe.

Cut one Back, matching the center back line to a dominant vertical stripe and matching horizontal stripes to the Front along the side seamline from the lower edge to the waist edge. Flip this Back over to cut the second Back, matching stripes.

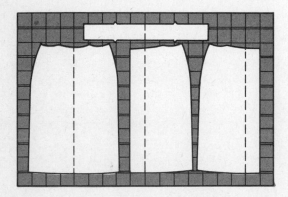

Straight Skirt without Pleat

To eliminate the back pleat in the straight skirt, cut *two* Fronts, one Waistband, and *no* Backs when you cut your fabric. Use one of the Fronts for the back of your skirt. Sew the skirt according to the instructions given for the skirt in the previous part of this chapter *except* skip the steps referring to the back seam and the pleat.

Straight Skirt with Slash

For a different effect, you may wish to sew the straight skirt with a slash rather than a pleat in the seam. To do this, you will omit the part of the Back pattern piece

allowed for a pleat. Instead, trace the Back with a ⅝-inch (1.6 cm) seam allowance along the center back line. Starting 1½ inches (3.8 cm) above the level of the dot, taper out to 2 inches (5.1 cm) past the center back line as illustrated. This extension will create a slash facing.

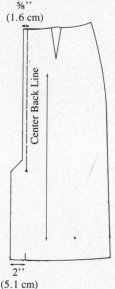

When you cut your fabric, cut two Backs as usual. Then sew the skirt according to the instructions given in the previous part of the chapter *except* disregard the instructions given under the headings "Back Seam" and "Hem." For these steps, follow the instructions below.

Back Seam

Backstitching securely at the dot, sew along the center back line from the dot to the waist edge.

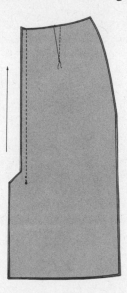

Press the seam open. Fold the slash facings to the wrong side in a line continuous with the center back seam and press.

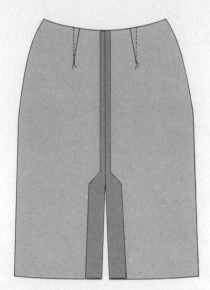

Hem

Fold the slash facings along the foldline right sides together with the skirt. Stitch across each facing along the 2-inch (5.1 cm) hemline.

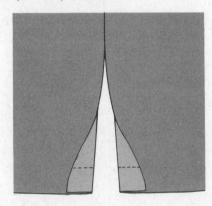

Trim the facing hem allowance to ⅜ inch (1.0 cm) from the stitching as illustrated.

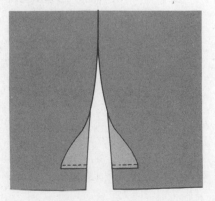

Turn the facings to their finished position. Then press in a 2-inch (5.1 cm) hem at the lower edge of the skirt. Bond or hand catchstitch the hem and the slash facings in place.

Straight Skirt with Center Front Pleat

One of the features of Pattern No. 445 is that the straight skirt can very easily be sewn so you can wear the pleat in front for a really sharp look.

Cut your fabric and sew the skirt together as usual *except* do not match the Waistband seam to the center back seam of the skirt since you will be wearing the pleat in front. Instead, match the Waistband seam to the side seam. Then, unless you are one of the few who need to trim the waist edge of the skirt for a better fit across your back, you will be able to wear the skirt with the pleat in front or in back.

Straight Skirt with Topstitched Pleat

In the straight skirt, the weight of the pleat fabric is secured by the Waistband so it's not necessary to topstitch the pleat as illustrated below to prevent it from drooping at the hemline. However, I often topstitch mine because I like the look of this traditional fashion detail.

To topstitch the pleat, use a straight stitch with 6 stitches per inch (4 mm stitch length). Start at the center back seam at the top of the pleat and topstitch for 2 inches (5.1 cm) at an angle as illustrated.

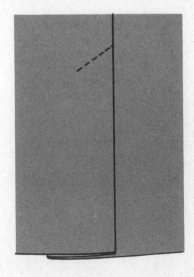

Chapter 8
Tank Swimsuit and Dolman Sleeve Cover-Up

Introduction

Imagine — making a swimsuit of your very own — one to really fit your figure! Swimsuits, especially one-piece swimsuits, are close-fitting garments so that if your figure deviates from the norm in any way, it's nearly impossible to purchase one that fits. For those of you who've had this experience, sewing your own suit gives you an extra advantage.

The swimsuit is one of the garments that I used to develop my *Ann Person*™ sewing methods. In the very beginning — before I had even found a swim fabric — I was trying a swimsuit. I used a stretchy piece of fabric that turned out to be wool double knit. It held up fine under the shower at home when I tested it. But I took it to Sun Valley on vacation, and each time I wore the swimsuit in the hot pool, it became tighter and tighter. By the end of the week, I had to buy a swimsuit because the one I'd made was beyond my getting into it. We are fortunate today to have wonderful *Antron** nylon/*Lycra** spandex for our swimsuits.

I will never forget the first swimsuit I ever sewed from swim fabric. My dad was visiting me that day. He lay down to take a nap on the davenport while I cut the suit out, and when he woke up an hour later, I had it on — much to his amazement. You'll be equally amazed at how simple it really is to sew the Stretch & Sew tank suit. And, by making the tank suit, you'll be learning the basic construction techniques for all other Stretch & Sew swimsuits.

I'm pleased that we've come such a long way in the design and style of our swimsuit patterns. The tank suit has sleek, vertical construction lines to flatter your figure. It's also wonderful for swimming — it's truly an action garment.

To top off your swimsuit you'll be sewing a dolman sleeve cover-up. Again, the construction couldn't be simpler. Once you've sewn the cover-up, you'll be inspired to try a dolman blouse or evening dress for fashion elegance.

*Registered trademarks of Du Pont

Tank Swimsuit and Dolman Sleeve Cover-Up

Pattern Selection

Stretch & Sew Pattern No. 1320

You'll be using *Stretch & Sew* Pattern No. 1320 to sew your tank suit. In this class we are featuring the tank suit with a full front lining. I'll share with you a technique for using the lining to enclose the seam allowances at the center front and along the side seams. The elastic application for finishing the garment edges will be a review of the turned-down elastic application you learned when you sewed your pants in Class 2.

Under "Special Information" at the end of the chapter, there are complete instructions for sewing bra cups instead of front lining into the suit. There are also instructions for omitting both bra cups and front lining.

Stretch & Sew Pattern No. 235

In this class you will be sewing a variation of *Stretch & Sew* Pattern No. 235. This pattern is for a loose-fitting dolman sleeve blouse or dress with a front neck slash. The neckline may be finished with Chanel trim extending into ties or with a collar. The sleeves, either short or three-quarter length, are finished with elastic in a casing.

The cover-up features the Chanel-trimmed neckline and short sleeves. The garment lower edges extend into points for a casual, poncho look. I have developed a way of cutting the cover-up on the bias from a 45-inch (114.3 cm) square of fabric. Then you get the extended points without using more yardage than required for View A which is only waist length.

Fabric Selection

Fabric for Your Tank Suit

Stretch & Sew Pattern No. 1320 was developed to be used with *Antron/Lycra* which has approximately 100 percent lengthwise stretch and 50 percent crosswise stretch. These two fibers, which were developed by Du Pont, are blended to form one yarn. *Lycra* gives the fabric its elasticity, causing it to conform perfectly to your figure. *Antron* is responsible for the brilliant colorations and the silken lustre of the fabric. It's as if a recipe were developed for the perfect swim fabric and *Antron* and *Lycra* were selected as the chief ingredients.

Fabric for Your Dolman Sleeve Cover-Up

Your swim cover-up may be sewn in a variety of fabrics. I personally enjoy sewing a cover-up in *Antron/Lycra* to match my swimsuit. Then my cover-up doubles as a dressy blouse over coordinating pants. Other possibilities for your cover-up are knit terry, cotton single knit, cotton interlock, or velour.

Yardage and Notions

After you have selected your swim fabric, refer to the back of the Pattern No. 1320 envelope for yardage and notions. Unlike most *Stretch & Sew* patterns, yardage for Pattern No. 1320 has been figured for fabrics without nap. This means that the layouts in the pattern instructions and in this chapter show the pattern pieces running in two directions. When you cut *Antron/Lycra*, nap is not a concern and the two-way layout saves you considerable yardage. If you select a swim fabric with a one-way design that requires the pattern pieces to be positioned in the same direction, your teacher will help you determine any additional yardage you may need.

For the dolman sleeve cover-up you will need 1-1/3 yards (1.22 m) of fabric, a 9-inch (22.9 cm) by 11-inch (27.9 cm) piece of *Do-Sew*® pattern material for a stay, and 1 yard (0.91 m) of *Stretch & Sew*™ ⅜-inch (1.0 cm) elastic.

Do not pretreat the elastic for your swimsuit because shrinking will compensate for the slight amount of relaxation which occurs when you stitch through the elastic. However, the elastic for your cover-up will be loose in a casing and requires pretreating. Pretreat it by soaking it in hot water and drying it in your dryer.

131

Tank Suit with Front Lining

Preparing Your Pattern

Determining Your Pattern Size

Refer to the back of the Pattern No. 1320 envelope and choose the size that corresponds to your bust measurement. Check the measurement chart to determine any necessary pattern adjustments.

Tracing Your Pattern Pieces

For the tank suit with a front lining, you will need to trace a Front and a Back. If you are tracing the pattern pieces up or down in size at the hip, taper back to your regular size along the leg edge as shown by the shading in the illustrations. Then you will be making a horizontal fit adjustment without changing the vertical length allowed for your size.

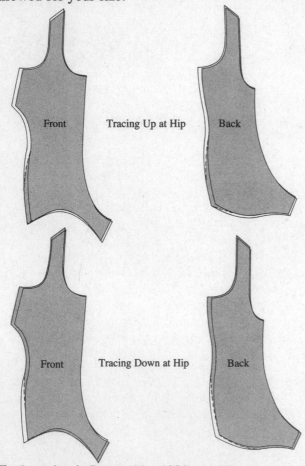

Front   Tracing Up at Hip   Back

Front   Tracing Down at Hip   Back

The bust dart in Pattern No. 1320 provides the same fit as the bust dart in the Basic Dress and Blouse Pattern No. 1505. In other words, if you found it necessary to lengthen, shorten, raise, or lower the dart when you prepared your basic dress pattern for Class 4, make the

same adjustment for your swimsuit bust dart. If you need to refresh your memory, refer to the section "Bust Dart Adjustment" in Chapter Four. There you will find the Standard High Point Measurements Chart as well as complete instructions for making an adjustment.

If you found that no bust dart adjustment was necessary when you prepared your basic dress pattern, the dart for your size in Pattern No. 1320 will fit your figure. The dart drawn on the Front pattern piece is for size 30 only. To draw in the dart for other sizes, mark the dot given for your size. Then draw lines from the dot to the corresponding notches on the side of the pattern. Transfer all other pattern markings to your tracing material.

A one-piece swimsuit must match the length of your torso for a comfortable and attractive fit. To be sure your swimsuit fits you in length, take an "overall body measurement." This is an awkward measurement to take yourself, so I suggest you have someone else do it to ensure the greatest possible accuracy. The measurement is taken from the hollow at the front natural neckline, down through the crotch, and up to the cervical bone at the back natural neckline.

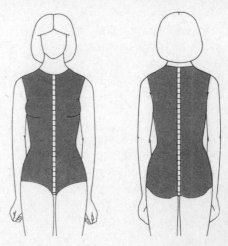

The full front lining stabilizes the swimsuit, causing it to require additional ease. To provide this ease, *add 1 inch (2.5 cm) to your overall body measurement.* Then compare it to the measurement given for your bust size on the chart below:

Bust Size	Overall Body Measurement
30	53 inches (134.6 cm)
32	54 inches (137.2 cm)
34	55 inches (139.7 cm)
36	56 inches (142.2 cm)
38	57 inches (144.8 cm)
40	58 inches (147.3 cm)
42	59 inches (149.9 cm)
44	60 inches (152.4 cm)

If the measurements are the same, your swimsuit pattern does not need a length adjustment. If the measurements are not the same, divide the difference between measurements in fourths. Then adjust both the Front and Back pattern pieces this amount on each shorten/lengthen line.

For example, if your own overall body measurement is 53 inches (134.6 cm), add 1 inch (2.5 cm) for extra ease to get 54 inches (137.2 cm). Then, if the chart measurement for your size is 56 inches (142.2 cm), your own measurement would be 2 inches (5.1 cm) less. Divide this amount in fourths to get 1/2 inch (1.3 cm). Slash and lap the Front and Back pattern pieces 1/2 inch (1.3 cm) at each shorten/lengthen line.

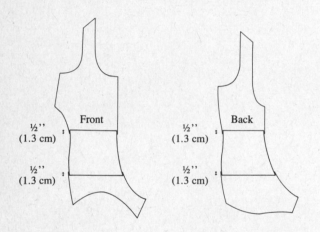

Or, if your own overall body measurement is 58 inches (147.3 cm), add 1 inch (2.5 cm) for extra ease to get 59 inches (149.9 cm). Then, if the chart measurement for your size is 56 inches (142.2 cm), your own measurement would be 3 inches (7.6 cm) greater. Divide this amount in fourths to get 3/4 inch (1.9 cm). Slash and spread the Front and Back pattern pieces 3/4 inch (1.9 cm) at each shorten/lengthen line. Back the openings with strips of pattern material.

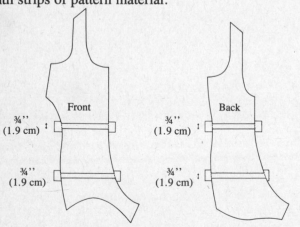

Cutting Your Fabric

Pretreating

Pretreat the *Antron/Lycra* you have selected for your swimsuit by machine-washing it in cool water and line-drying. Do not pretreat the elastic for your swimsuit.

Cutting Garment Pieces

From your swim fabric you will need to cut two Fronts and two Backs. *Antron/Lycra* is knit so the greater stretch in the fabric is vertical rather than horizontal as it is in most knit fabrics. But the greater amount of stretch must still go across the pattern — around the body in the finished garment. First you will need to refold the fabric to make it possible for the greater stretch to go across the pattern when you are cutting through a double thickness.

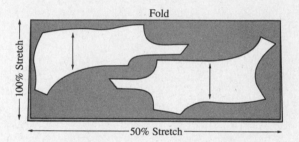

If you're cutting through a single thickness at a time, turn each pattern piece over to cut the second piece so you will have a right side and a left side for your swimsuit.

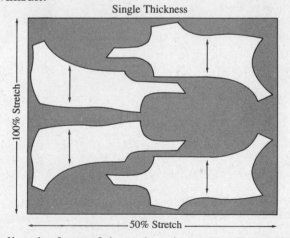

To line the front of the swimsuit, cut two Fronts from swim lining fabric. Place the pattern pieces on the fabric so the greater stretch will go around the body in the finished garment.

Transfer all construction marks to your swim fabric and lining. The seam allowances on your swimsuit pattern are ¼ inch (0.6 cm) wide and the seams will be stretched firmly as you sew them. To ensure strong seams, do not clip into the seam allowances at the notches. Instead, cut wedges outside the seam allowance or use your *Stretch & Sew™* fabric marker to indicate notches.

The elastic for your swimsuit will be cut during construction.

Sewing Your Tank Suit

Unless otherwise indicated, stitch seams right sides together with a ¼-inch (0.6 cm) seam allowance. Use a straight stitch with 9 stitches per inch (3 mm stitch length). Because of the close fit of swimsuits and the stretchiness of swim fabric, all seams are stress seams. Stretch as you sew and, for reinforcement, backstitch at the beginning and end of each seam. When I use "right" and "left," I'm referring to the finished garment as if you were wearing it.

Darts

On the Front pieces fold each bust dart along the center and pin. Sew the darts, starting at the notches and stitching in a straight line to the point. Then tie off the threads at the point of each dart. Trim the darts to ¼ inch (0.6 cm) from the stitching and finger-press the darts down.

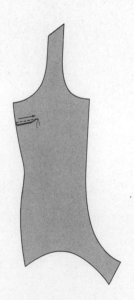

Follow the same procedure to sew the bust darts on the Front lining pieces.

Center Seams and Side Seams

Beginning at the lower edge, pin and stitch the Front pieces together along the center front. Stretch the swimsuit seams firmly as you sew because you want them to be as elastic as the swimsuit itself.

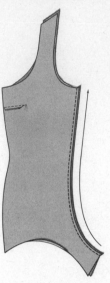

In the same way, pin and stitch the Backs together along the center back. Then doublestitch the center back seam for reinforcement by sewing a second row of stitching on the seam allowance ⅛ inch (0.3 cm) from the previous stitching.

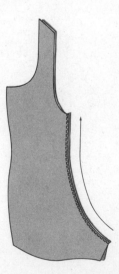

Next, beginning at the lower edge, pin and stitch each side seam.

Full Front Lining

Place the Front lining pieces right sides together. Then open out the swimsuit so the Fronts are right sides together. Place the Front linings on the left Front of the swimsuit. Pin the Front linings in place along the center front seam. Beginning at the lower edge, stitch over the previous stitching line through all four layers.

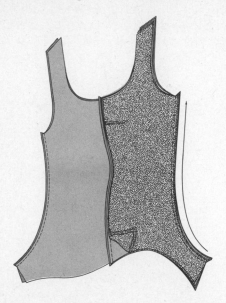

To enclose the seam allowances at the right side seam, wrap the right Front lining around the left Front to the right Back, rolling the swimsuit up inside. The right side of the Front lining should be against the wrong side of the Back. Pin and stitch over the previous stitching line.

Turn the right Front lining right side out. Then repeat the procedure to enclose the seam allowances at the left side seam. Wrap the left Front lining around the right Front to the left Back, rolling the swimsuit up inside. The right side of the Front lining should be against the wrong side of the Back. Pin and stitch over the previous stitching line. Turn the left Front lining right side out.

Now you can see how clean and finished the enclosed seam allowances are. Congratulations on mastering this technique!

Crotch and Shoulder Seams

Pin and stitch the crotch seam, including the Front lining and using a ⅝-inch (1.6 cm) seam allowance. Then trim the seam allowance of the Back piece only to ¼ inch (0.6 cm) and finger-press all seam allowances toward the Back.

Stitch ⅜ inch (1.0 cm) from the previous stitching through all layers. Trim the excess seam allowance to ⅛ inch (0.3 cm) from the stitching.

Treating the lining and the swim fabric as one, pin each set of shoulder straps right sides together, matching widths along the seamline. Stitch them with a ¼-inch (0.6 cm) seam allowance.

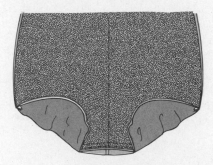

Finger-press the shoulder seams open.

Leg Elastic

The elastic application you will use to finish the edges of your swimsuit is basically the same technique as the turned-down elastic finish you learned in Class 2 to finish the waist of the pants and the four-gore skirt. As you apply the elastic to the suit, treat the lining and swim fabric as one.

Measure a leg opening of the swimsuit along the cut edge, taking care not to stretch the fabric. Subtract 2 inches (5.1 cm). Then cut two strips of *Stretch & Sew*

⅜-inch (1.0 cm) elastic this length. Lap the ends of one strip ½ inch (1.3 cm), forming a circle, and stitch them together securely.

Neckline and Armhole Elastic

Measure the neckline of the swimsuit and cut a strip of ⅜-inch (1.0 cm) elastic this length. Lap the ends of the strip ½ inch (1.3 cm) and stitch them together securely. Then divide the elastic in fourths and mark the divisions with pins.

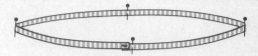

Next, with a 1:1 ratio, pin the elastic to the wrong side of the *Front* leg opening even with the cut edge. Pin the remaining elastic across the Back leg opening, distributing the fullness of the suit evenly.

Next, divide the neckline of the swimsuit in fourths and mark the divisions with pins. Pin the elastic to the neckline, matching quarter divisions.

With the elastic on top and the swimsuit next to the sewing maching, zigzag close to the edge of the leg opening, stretching the elastic to fit the Back of the swimsuit.

Zigzag the elastic to the neck edge. Then fold the elastic toward the wrong side of the swimsuit and pin it in place. Zigzag the neckline again with the zigzag stitch just overlapping the edge of the elastic.

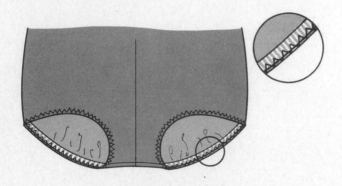

Measure an armhole of the swimsuit and cut two strips of ⅜-inch (1.0 cm) elastic this length. Apply the elastic to the armhole openings, following the same procedure as described for the neckline elastic. That's it! Your swimsuit is ready for the pool or beach.

Fold the elastic toward the wrong side of the swimsuit and pin it in place. Keep the fabric pulled straight and taut with the edge of the elastic right against the fold of the fabric. Zigzag the leg opening again with the zigzag stitch just overlapping the edge of the elastic as illustrated. Finish the second leg opening in the same way.

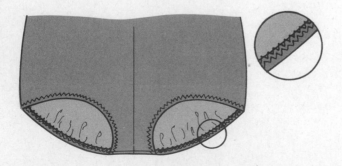

The Dolman Sleeve Cover-up

Preparing Your Pattern

Determining Your Pattern Size

Pattern No. 235 has a very free and easy fit. Because the cover-up does not have a waistline, size Medium fits all figures through bust size 44 without any pattern adjustments ever being necessary. When you trace size Medium, you will be able to cut the fabric on the bias as I'll describe below for the best use of your yardage.

Tracing Your Pattern Pieces

For your dolman sleeve cover-up, trace a Front/Back in size Medium, following the ''Cutting Lines for View A.'' You will also need to trace a Front Facing (View A & B), and a Front Neck Template. Transfer the pattern markings to your tracing material.

Cutting Your Fabric

Pretreating

Pretreat the fabric you have selected for your dolman sleeve cover-up, following the care instructions which accompany the fabric. Pretreat *Stretch & Sew* ⅜-inch (1.0 cm) elastic by soaking it in hot water and drying it in your dryer.

Cutting Garment Pieces

First cut a Chanel strip 1⅝ inches (4.1 cm) wide by 45 inches (114.3 cm) long for the neckline trim. *Antron/Lycra* has enough stretch running in each direction that Chanel strips may be cut either way. In this case, cut *Antron/Lycra* with the greater stretch running the width of the strip. Then you will be able to maintain the width of your yardage for cutting the Front/Back piece. For other fabrics, which are generally wider, cut the Chanel strip with the greater stretch running the length of the strip.

For the Front/Back, start with a 45-inch (114.3 cm) square of fabric. I have devised a way of folding this square to create a pointed hemline at the front and back

of the cover-up without wasting any fabric. First fold the square diagonally, forming a triangle.

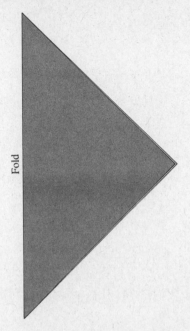

Then fold the triangle in half to form a smaller triangle as illustrated.

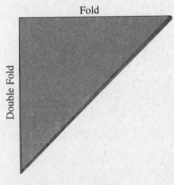

Now place the Front/Back pattern piece on the fabric, matching the shoulder line to the fold of the triangle and the center front/center back line to the double fold.

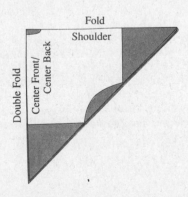

To cut out the Front/Back, you should cut the neck edge, the sleeve edge, and the underarm curve. Don't cut along the pattern lower edge.

Remove the pattern piece and unfold the Front/Back once only. Pin the Front Neck Template to the Front, matching neck edges and center fronts.

Using the Template as a guide, cut the neckline on the Front.

Use the scraps of fabric from the square to cut a Front Facing (View A & B). You will also need to cut a Front Facing (View A & B) from *Do-Sew*. The fabric piece will be the actual facing and the piece from *Do-Sew* will be the Stay for the front neckline slash.

Transfer all construction marks to your fabric and Stay.

Sewing Your Dolman Sleeve Cover-Up

Unless otherwise indicated, stitch seams right sides together with a ⅝-inch (1.6 cm) seam allowance. Use a straight stitch with 9 stitches per inch (3 mm stitch length) and stretch as you sew. For reinforcement, I recommend that you backstitch at the beginning and end of each seam. Remember that by ''right'' and ''left,'' I am referring to the finished garment as if you were wearing it.

Front Facing

The neckline of your dolman sleeve cover-up features a slash opening that accomplishes the same thing as the tab front — basically it allows you to pull the garment over your head. However, the slash opening creates a different look, giving you an extra design dimension for your sewing. Notice that the Stay serves the same purpose as it did for the tab front. It guides your stitching and stabilizes the fabric to create an even, professional-looking slash.

First mark the center fronts on the Front and the Front Facing with a *light* crease or pins. Then place the Stay against the wrong side of the Front Facing, matching edges and center fronts.

Next, with right sides together, pin the Front Facing to the Front, matching neck edges and center front markings. With 12 stitches per inch (2.5 mm stitch length), sew along the slash stitching line through all three layers. Begin your stitching at the neck edge and sew toward the point of the slash. To make turning easier, sew one stitch across the point. Then sew to the neck edge on the other slash stitching line.

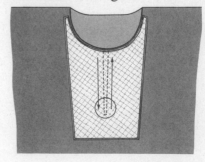
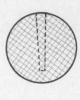

Trim the *Do-Sew* to ⅛ inch (0.3 cm) from the stitching. Now cut down the center of the slash through all three layers — be careful not to cut through your stitching.

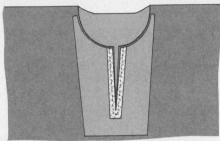

Turn the Front Facing to the wrong side of the garment and press, rolling the seams slightly to the underside. (If you are working with *Antron/Lycra,* I suggest you use a press cloth and set your iron in the synthetic range. Excessive heat will damage this fabric.) Pin the Facing in place along the neck edge.

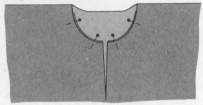

Chanel Trim and Ties

During Class 4 you learned the fundamentals of my Chanel trim application. Now, as you sew your cover-up, you will learn how to finish a garment edge with Chanel trim that extends to form ties. This technique is one attractive way to finish a neck edge that has a slash.

Begin by placing the Chanel strip right sides together with the left Front neck edge, allowing 13 inches (33.0 cm) of the strip to extend beyond the slash for a tie. With the Chanel strip on top and the garment next to the sewing machine, stitch the strip to the neckline, using a ⅜-inch (1.0 cm) seam allowance. You should not stretch the neck edge of the garment, but stretch the strip slightly to eliminate the slack in the fabric.

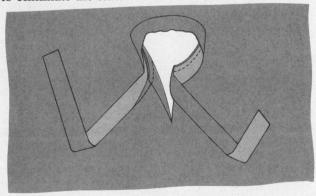

Cut the remaining end of the strip 13 inches (33.0 cm) from the edge of the slash for the other tie. Carefully press the Chanel strip and the seam allowances toward the neck opening. On each side of the slash, clip the seam allowance of the Chanel strip to the stitching. You will see how this clipping releases the seam allowance of the Chanel strip, making it possible to sew the seams of the ties.

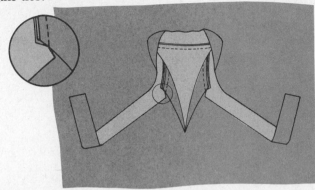

Fold each tie right sides together. Beginning at the clip, stitch along the center of the tie. It's important that you stretch these seams firmly as you sew so they are able to withstand the stress of being tied and untied.

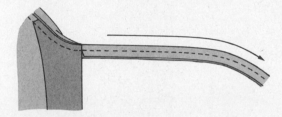

Turn the ties right side out, using a safety pin or a loop turner. Then you will finish the Chanel trim just as you learned to do when you sewed the basic dress.

First fold the Chanel strip over the seam allowances to the wrong side of the garment. The fold of the trim should be right against the cut edges of the seam allowances. Pin the trim in place. To secure the trim, stitch-in-the-ditch by sewing into the seamline on the right side of the garment. Catch the trim on the underside in your stitching.

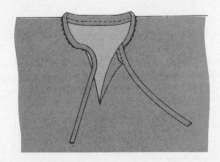

On the wrong side of the garment, trim the extra Chanel strip to ⅛ inch (0.3 cm) from the stitching. To finish the ends of the ties, you may tie a knot at each end or you may fold the cut edges into the ends and handstitch them.

Side Seams

Beginning ½ inch (1.3 cm) from the garment lower edge, pin and stitch each side seam. Doublestitch the underarm portion of the seam as illustrated by sewing a second row of stitching on the seam allowance ⅛ inch (0.3 cm) from the previous stitching.

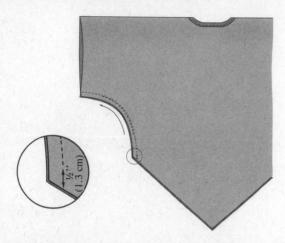

Trim the side seams to ⅜ inch (1.0 cm), leaving the sleeve edges full width as illustrated.

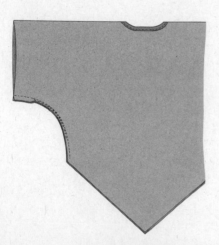

Press the seams open at the sleeve and garment lower edges.

Sleeve Finish

The sleeves of the cover-up are finished with elastic in a casing. I have developed a technique which encloses the elastic while you stitch the casing.

For the casing, turn ⅞ inch (2.2 cm) at the lower edge of the sleeve to the wrong side and press. Then sew a row of stitching ⅛ inch (0.3 cm) from the fold.

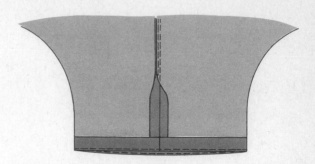

To determine the correct length of *Stretch & Sew* ⅜-inch (1.0 cm) elastic, measure around your upper arm. Mark off this much elastic but do not cut it.

With the edge of the elastic close to the stitching, pin the end of the elastic to the sleeve at the seam as illustrated.

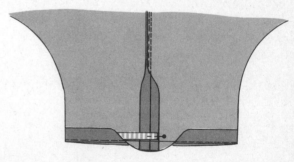

To enclose the elastic, I suggest you use a zipper foot. Sew a second row of stitching ⅝ inch (1.6 cm) from the fold of the casing, beginning and ending 1½ inches (3.8 cm) from the seamline. Do not catch the elastic in your stitching.

Pull the elastic through the casing until the mark appears. Cut the elastic at the mark. Then lap the ends of the elastic ½ inch (1.3 cm) and stitch securely.

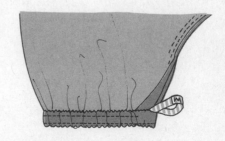

Stitch across the opening in the casing ⅝ inch (1.6 cm) from the fold, overlapping the previous stitching.

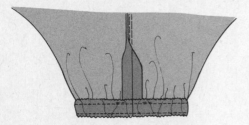

Finish the second sleeve edge in the same manner as you finished the first one.

Hem Finish

First you will miter the point on the front of your cover-up. To do this, fold the point right sides together along the center front line. Next measure along the fold ⅜ inch (1.0 cm) from the point and mark a dot. Then measure along the cut edges ¾ inch (1.9 cm) from the point and mark a second dot. Connect the dots by a line of stitching.

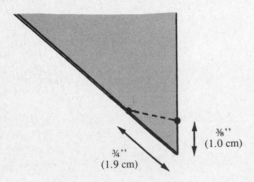

Trim the seam allowance ⅛ inch (0.3 cm) from the stitching.

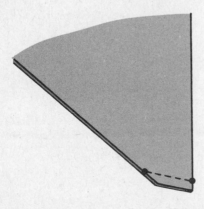

Miter the point on the back of the cover-up in the same way as the front. Then turn all lower edges ⅜ inch (1.0 cm) to the wrong side. Topstitch ¼ inch (0.6 cm) from the folded edges. Give your cover-up a final pressing and you're ready for the beach!

Special Information

Tank Suit with Bra Cups

We developed Pattern No. 1320 so the tank suit may be sewn with bra cups. For a suit with bra cups, refer to the back of the Pattern No. 1320 envelope for View A yardage and notions. You will notice that View A requires less swim lining than View B. This is because the full front lining is not necessary in a swim suit with bra cups. You will be cutting a Crotch Lining only. For View A you will need ⅝ yard (0.57 m) of felt-backed elastic and bra cups from your *Stretch & Sew Fabrics*® center.

Preparing Your Pattern

Trace a Front and a Back as described previously for the tank suit with a front lining — *except* do *not* add 1 inch (2.5 cm) to your overall body measurement before comparing it to the measurement for your size on the Overall Body Measurement Chart. Without the full front lining in your swimsuit, you do not need the extra ease provided by the inch. You will also need to trace a Crotch Lining pattern piece.

Cutting Garment Pieces

From your swim fabric, cut two Fronts and two Backs. Refer to the cutting instructions for the tank suit with a front lining if you need to refresh your memory on refolding *Antron/Lycra* so the greater stretch will go around the body in the finished garment.

From swim lining fabric, cut one Crotch Lining.

Darts and Center Seams

Pin and stitch the bust darts on the Fronts, starting at the notches and sewing in a straight line toward the point. Then tie off the threads at the point of each dart. Trim the darts to ¼ inch (0.6 cm) from the stitching and finger-press the darts down.

Beginning at the lower edge, pin and stitch the Fronts together along the center front with a ¼-inch (0.6 cm) seam allowance. Remember to stretch firmly as you sew this seam and all other seams of the suit. For reinforcement, doublestitch the seam by sewing a second row of stitching on the seam allowance ⅛ inch (0.3 cm) from the previous stitching.

In the same manner, pin and stitch the Backs together along the center back. Doublestitch.

Crotch, Side, and Shoulder Seams

Pin and stitch the crotch seam, using a ⅝-inch (1.6 cm) seam allowance. Next place the right side of the Crotch Lining over the Back and pin, keeping all edges even. Sew over the previous stitching.

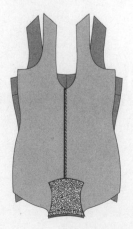

Trim the seam allowance of the Back piece only to ¼ inch (0.6 cm). Then fold the Crotch Lining to the Front, enclosing the seam allowances. Stitch ⅜ inch (1.0 cm) from the seam through all layers. Trim the extending seam allowances and pin the Crotch Lining even with the edges of the leg openings.

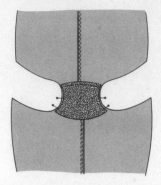

Beginning at the lower edge, pin and stitch each side seam. Doublestitch these seams.

Pin and stitch each set of shoulder straps right sides together, matching widths along the seamline.

Finger-press the shoulder seams open.

Leg Elastic

Measure a leg opening of the swimsuit along the cut edge, taking care not to stretch the fabric. Subtract 2 inches (5.1 cm). Then cut two strips of *Stretch & Sew* ⅜-inch (1.0 cm) elastic this length. Lap the ends of one strip ½ inch (1.3 cm), forming a circle, and stitch them together securely.

Next, with a 1:1 ratio, pin the elastic to the wrong side of the *Front* leg opening even with the cut edge. Pin the remaining elastic across the Back leg opening, distributing the fullness of the suit evenly.

With the elastic on top and the swimsuit next to the sewing maching, zigzag close to the edge of the leg opening, stretching the elastic to fit the Back of the swimsuit.

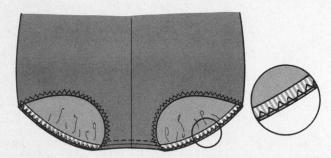

Fold the elastic toward the wrong side of the swimsuit and pin it in place. Keep the fabric pulled straight and taut with the edge of the elastic right against the fold of the fabric. Zigzag the leg opening again with the zigzag stitch just overlapping the edge of the elastic as illustrated. Finish the second leg opening in the same way.

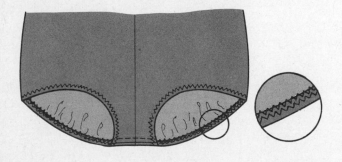

Neckline and Armhole Elastic

Measure the neckline of the swimsuit and cut a strip of ⅜-inch (1.0 cm) elastic this length. Lap the ends of the strip ½ inch (1.3 cm) and stitch them together securely. Then divide the elastic in fourths and mark the divisions with pins.

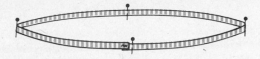

Next divide the neckline of the swimsuit in fourths and mark the divisions with pins. Pin the elastic to the neckline, matching quarter divisions.

Zigzag the elastic to the neck edge, but *do not turn the elastic to the inside for the second stitching at this time.* You will complete the elastic after you have applied the bra cups.

Measure an armhole of the swimsuit and cut two strips of ⅜-inch (1.0 cm) elastic this length. Apply the elastic to the armhole openings, following the same procedure as described for the neckline elastic. Do not turn the elastic to the inside for the second stitching at this time.

Bra Cups

First trim the lining from the inside of the bra cups close to the stitching. Then invert the bra cups to make them easier to work with. With a 1:1 ratio, pin the strip of felt-backed elastic along the lower edge of the bra cups so the felt side of the elastic will be against the body in the finished suit. Zigzag along the upper edge of the elastic, securing it to the lining.

Trim the lining to ⅛ inch (0.3 cm) from the stitching.

If you are making the swimsuit for yourself, try it on, fitting the bra cups into place under the Front. Smooth the lining and pin it in position along the neck and armhole edges and at the center front as illustrated.

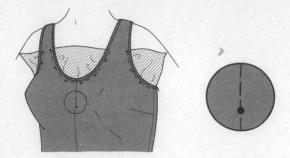

If you are making the swimsuit for someone else, position the bra cups behind the Front so that the point of the dart is directed toward the high point of the bra cup. Smooth the lining and pin it in place as described above.

Set your sewing machine at its widest and longest zigzag stitch to zigzag-baste along the middle of the elastic at the Front neck and armhole edges. Do not remove the pin at the center front.

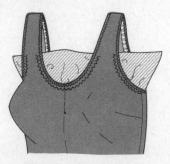

Turn the swimsuit wrong side out and invert the bra cups again. Pin the felt-backed elastic to the suit at the center front. Then smooth the lining and the felt-backed elastic toward the side seams and pin it in place. At the side seams, sew over the previous stitching as illustrated. For reinforcement, be sure to backstitch on the felt-backed elastic.

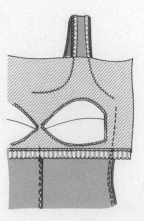

Trim the felt-backed elastic and the excess lining even with the side seam allowances and the neck and armhole edges.

Neckline and Armhole Elastic Finish

At the neckline and armholes, fold the elastic toward the wrong side of the swimsuit and pin it in place. Zigzag with the zigzag stitch just overlapping the edge of the elastic.

Natural-Look Tank Suit

If you choose a medium- to dark-colored swim fabric, you may wish to sew the tank suit without bra cups or front lining. Simply prepare your pattern and sew the suit according to the instructions for the tank suit with bra cups, omitting the bra cup application.

Index

Notes

Care Instruction

black ◁1▷ Machine wash, warm.

◁2▷ Machine wash, warm; line dry,

red ◁3▷ Machine wash, warm; tumble dry, remove promptly.

◁4▷ Machine wash, warm; delicate cycle; tumble dry, low use cool iron.

◁5▷ Machine wash warm; do not dry clean,

◁6▷ Hand Hand wash, separately,

◁7▷ Dry clean only.

(8) Dry clean pile fabric method only

◁9▷ Wipe with damp cloth only.

Notes

Notes

Notes